HOW TO FOOL YOUR PARENTS

25 BRAIN-BREAKING
MAGIC TRICKS

By **DAVID KWONG**
Illustrated by **MICHAEL KORFHAGE**

HARPER
An Imprint of HarperCollinsPublishers

Special thanks to the smartest people in the room—Dave Shukan, Francis Menotti, and John Stessel—for your invaluable help in putting this book together.

How to Fool Your Parents: 25 Brain-Breaking Magic Tricks
Text copyright © 2024 by David Kwong
Illustrations copyright © 2024 by Michael Korfhage
All rights reserved. Printed in Canada.
No part of this book may be used or reproduced in any manner whatsoever without written permission except in the case of brief quotations embodied in critical articles and reviews. For information address HarperCollins Children's Books, a division of HarperCollins Publishers, 195 Broadway, New York, NY 10007.
www.harpercollinschildrens.com

Library of Congress Control Number: 2023948484
ISBN 978-0-06-314058-5

Typography by Julia Tyler
24 25 26 27 28 TC 10 9 8 7 6 5 4 3 2
First Edition

To Ashley-Brooke and Cozy

You've brought more magic into my life than I ever could have imagined.

—D.K.

TABLE OF CONTENTS

Who's the Smartest One of All?   1

The Magician's Oath   5

The Most Important Thing in Magic   9

Tricky Terminology   13

Part One: Sleight of Hand   **19**

    ☞ The Hand Is Quicker . . .   21

Part Two: Technological Trickery   **65**

    ☞ Digital Deception   67

Part Three: Mentalism   **109**

    ☞ Mind Over Matter   111

Part Four: Covert Communication   **147**

    ☞ "Now you *say* it, now you don't!"   149

My BRAIN is the KEY that sets me FREE.

—HARRY HOUDINI

WHO'S THE SMARTEST ONE OF ALL?

WHEN I WAS seven years old, my father took me to a farm to pick a pumpkin for Halloween. After I had selected the perfect pumpkin to carve into a jack-o'-lantern, we spotted a magician standing in front of the barn. I remember exactly what he looked like: he was bald, wore big round glasses, and sported the warmest, friendliest smile. Most important, he had a bunny rabbit!

The magician performed a trick that would change my life forever. He showed us two sponge balls. Taking one and placing it in my father's hand, the magician told him to close his fist tightly around it. Next, he held up the second sponge ball and with a wave of his hand it vanished. My father then opened his hand to reveal both of the sponge balls. I turned to him and asked him how the trick worked. My father flashed me a sheepish grin. He was both amused and perplexed at the same time. "I have absolutely no idea," he said. *My father had been fooled.* And that's when I knew I wanted to be a magician.

I was shocked that my dad couldn't figure out the trick because he is smart. *Really* smart. My mom too. They are both university professors. But all that intelligence goes out the window when a magician sets the rules. When you learn magic, you'll be a step ahead. You'll control the angles. You'll have secret codes that only you and your friends know. You think your parents are smart? The magician is smarter.

I've spent my entire life learning thousands of tricks, or, as the professionals call them, "effects." And I've selected the best ones—illusions and secret codes that will astound, amaze, and confuse—to share them with you. Some of them I loved doing as a kid, and others are brand-new, using today's technology. But all of them allow you to mess with people's expectations of how the world functions, the rules that run our lives.

And no one makes more rules than your parents. Most of them are important, like "Don't skip school" or "Don't put your dog in the washing machine." But some of them are annoying, like "You can't eat ice cream for dinner." When I was a kid, I loved magic because it allowed me to be the one in charge of my parents' attention, their actions, even their thoughts sometimes. When you perform magic, your parents have to play by *your rules*.

The following pages contain professional secrets that have been passed down through generations of magicians. Make sure your parents do not read this book! These secrets are now yours and yours alone. Master these tricks and you will be the smartest person in the room.

Have fun fooling your parents!

NEVER REVEAL THE SECRET.

NEVER REPEAT a TRICK.

PRACTICE, PRACTICE, PRACTICE! BEFORE PERFORMING a TRICK.

4

THE MAGICIAN'S OATH

IN THIS BOOK I am going to let you in on some of the best tricks from the magician's vault of secrets. These effects are built on principles of illusion that magicians have been guarding for centuries! So, before you dive in, I need you to take the following oath. Turn the page, place your right hand on the book, raise your left, and say:

MAGICIAN'S OATH

I, _____, will
(Print Your Name Here)

1 never reveal the secret (especially to my parents),

2 never repeat a trick, and

3 practice, practice, practice before performing a trick.

_____
(Sign Here)

_____
(Date Here)

CERTIFIED
by the
SECRET
ORDER

1   This one is self-explanatory. The essence of a magic trick is that you know something your parents don't know. Keep that secret to yourself and relish knowing that you can fool your folks, especially when the secret is simple!

2   Why? So much of magic relies on the element of surprise. If you repeat a trick, your audience will know what to look for. If your parents ask to see something again, it's best to say, "Let me show you something else" and do another trick.

3   It's important that you rehearse these tricks after you learn them. If you're not smooth, your parents will notice the cracks! Try practicing in front of a mirror or filming yourself with a cell phone. If you are effortless, your effects will truly seem magical!

THE MOST IMPORTANT THING IN MAGIC

MAGIC IS NOTHING without a good performance. You have one single goal when you do magic, and that is to get your parents to *believe* that you have superpowers.

The reality is that the secrets behind most magic tricks are simple: you have two coins instead of one; you "forced" them to pick a playing card; you had a friend in on the trick. But a good performance distances your audience from the truth.

Let me give you an example: say you're doing a mind-reading trick. Your parents have chosen a playing card and you already know what it is. What you don't want to do is merely reveal their card. Instead, look them deep in their eyes and murmur an incantation that you learned from an old one-eyed mystic. Or touch their foreheads and sense the magnetic energy that is emitted from their thoughts, a technique taught to you by a wandering faith healer. Of course, it's all baloney, but if you can get them to think that something supernatural is going on, they will never suspect that you knew the card already.

You'll be more fun to watch too! Think of every trick as a mini one-person play. There's the setup, in which you introduce the impossible task; the middle, in which you attempt the feat with dexterity and sheer will; and the astonishing finish, as you succeed against all odds!

If you can get your parents to believe, you'll amaze yourself about what you can get away with.

The MAGICIAN is an ACTOR playing the part of a MAGICIAN.

—JEAN-EUGÈNE ROBERT-HOUDIN

TRICKY TERMINOLOGY

HERE IS A LIST OF TERMS that you will learn in this book. The best tricks mix and match these moves and principles to make extra-deceptive tricks.

Ditch: Ditching is when you secretly dispose of an object. Ditching doesn't have to happen quickly. If you secretly have a coin in your hand, go to your case to pick up your wand and leave the coin.

Ending Clean: You have ended clean when you are able to get rid of the evidence of how the trick worked. If you have a duplicate card, for example, you end clean when you find a moment to sneak that card into your pocket.

Force: When you force your audience member, you are making them select something when they think they have free choice. Through clever methods, anything can be forced, from cards to coins to numbers.

Frame: For magic through the camera, the frame is what the audience will see on the screen. Often, the moves happen outside the frame, where your audience can't see your secret preparations.

Gimmick: A gimmick is an unseen part of a prop that makes the trick work. If something has been gimmicked, it's been rigged to have a secret function.

Impromptu: Some of the best magic tricks are "impromptu effects," meaning ones that are done spontaneously or without preparation. Magic can be at its most mind-blowing when you create miracles out of borrowed everyday items. You're not using special props, so the magic must be real!

Load: Secretly adding something to what you are already holding. If you have an index card and you sneak a second one behind it, you've loaded the second card.

Magician's Case: A magician's case is an essential. It allows you to have all your props and tricks ready at hand. But it also provides you with a place to hide objects or ditch them (remember ditching?). Grab a shoebox or an old suitcase and have fun adding some special magical touches to it.

Magician's Choice: Also known as *equivoque* (rhymes with "artichoke"), this is a very clever way of forcing one of three objects. The more items your parents can select from, the fairer the choice, right? Wrong!

Misdirection: The most important tool in magic! Misdirection is the art of making someone focus somewhere else, or even *think* of something else. It directs them away from the secret move you are performing. In "Coin Slam," picking up the book is the misdirection for secretly ditching the coin. Another way to think about it is that misdirection is the false reason for why you are doing something.

Multiple Methods: This refers to when a trick has many different layers of deception to it. If your parent cracks one secret, the others will still keep them guessing.

One Ahead: You are one ahead when you have already secretly accomplished a task. For example, you claim you will make a ball appear under a cup. But you have a secret second ball under the cup already. You are "one ahead" with that second ball. Now, simply make the first ball disappear and pretend that it is traveling invisibly to the cup.

Out: An out is the magician's backup plan. Tricks go wrong all the time. Don't panic! If you have an out ready, you can pivot the trick to a new direction. The best out? Laugh about the mistake and say, "Let me show you another trick." Above all, the show must go on!

Reveal: A reveal is when you show your audience something that was previously hidden or kept from them. The end of the trick often involves revealing that your prediction was right or that an object has traveled impossibly to a new location.

Steal: This is a sleight of hand move that allows you to obtain an object secretly. You can steal a coin out of a folded piece of paper, a ball from under a cup, or an extra playing card from your pocket. If the audience isn't seeing it, you're stealing!

Stooge: A stooge is a magician's secret helper. They're also known as plants, confederates, and conspirators. Most tricks don't use stooges, but sometimes it's best to work in a team and secretly communicate with one another!

Switch: A switch is when you swap one object for another. In your audience's eyes, nothing has happened. The two items appear the same and they were never aware of your secret move.

Time Misdirection: One way to take the heat off your secret moves is to distort *when* things are happening. If you put time in between when you do an important move and the result, your audience will not connect the two. For example, if you drop a coin behind a table, try stepping away from the table before showing that the coin is gone from your hand. Tell a joke. Laugh with your audience for twenty seconds. Your audience will forget that the table had anything to do with it!

PART ONE

SLEIGHT
OF HAND

THE HAND IS QUICKER . . .

PEOPLE HAVE BEEN fooling each other since the dawn of time. For example, the cups and balls, perhaps the most classic of all magic tricks, has been traced to ancient India, China, and Egypt. The Roman philosopher Seneca writes about the cups and balls in AD 65. That's almost two thousand years ago! It's perhaps the oldest sleight of hand trick in the world.

Sleight of hand is trickery using physical dexterity. For the cups and balls, the magician vanishes balls and makes them reappear underneath the cups using secret maneuvers. Usually, the performer finishes the trick by lifting up the cups to reveal bigger objects like lemons, limes, and oranges (I've even seen it done with baby chickens!). The cups-and-balls trick is a true test of a magician's ability to manipulate objects right under the audience's noses.

Have you ever heard the phrase "the hand is quicker than the eye"? That's sleight of hand! These tricks use sly moves like loading, switching, and ditching. The most important element of sleight of hand is misdirection. This is when you make your audience look away from where the secret move is happening.

In this chapter I will teach you some of my favorite illusions that will allow you to trick your parents with nothing but some simple everyday props and your own two hands. Let the fooling begin!

ICE CREAM FOR DINNER

I LOVE BROCCOLI. I know, I know, I am a strange person. To be clear, I love my dad's beef and broccoli, not gross, steamed, soggy broccoli. But the reason I would most look forward to my parents buying broccoli was for the really thick rubber band that holds it together. It's perfect for so many magic tricks!

In this trick, you are going to use your parents' assumptions against them. They are going to assume there's a single index card when you actually have two pieces. Your thick rubber band does all the dirty work.

This effect is based on a classic trick called Out to Lunch. In this version, you can use it to fool your parents into letting you skip your chores or eat ice cream for dinner.

The trick is easy. The hard part is coming up with what you want to fool your parents into giving you!

THE SECRET

A rubber band hides the fact that there are two index cards.

YOU'LL NEED

- A stack of index cards
- Scissors
- A thick rubber band
- A pen or pencil

Setup Step 2

THE SETUP

1. Remove a single index card and set it aside. Place a rubber band around the rest of the stack.

2. On half of the top card (A), above the rubber band, draw a speech bubble. Inside the bubble, write a secret phrase you want to fool your parent

with. You can write "You do not have to do your chores" or "I will give you $20." My favorite is "You can eat ice cream for dinner."

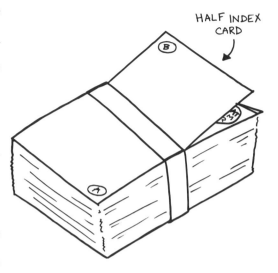

HALF INDEX CARD

3. Next, take the single index card and cut it neatly in half.

4. Place one half of it (B) on top of the card with the speech bubble, with the bottom of it going under the rubber band. Discard the other half. You can see the rubber band hides the seam and makes it look like there's a single blank card on top of the stack. Thick rubber bands are better for hiding the seam.

Setup Step 4

PERFORMANCE

1. Bring out your stack of index cards held together by a rubber band.

2. With your pen, above the rubber band, draw a speech bubble identical to the one you drew before. Inside it,

Performance Step 2

Performance Step 2

Performance Step 3

write something nice like, "Best parent in the world." Below the rubber band, draw a picture of your parent. Make it silly and fun! Then have your parent sign the picture. Your parent has now authorized this drawing!

3. To do the secret move, you are going to turn your wrist toward you to hide the faces of the cards from your audience. Grab the bottom of card (A) and pull the whole card out from underneath the half card (B). Use the fingers of your other hand to keep the half card on the top in place.

4. Once you have card (A) in your hand, put the stack of index cards away. The index card in your hand now has a picture of your parent saying your secret phase. But don't show this picture too

quickly. You have to sell the magic! Rub the card on the table as if you are miraculously transforming it, giving your parent a false explanation for what is happening. These theatrics make your parent focus on the magic and cause them to forget about the stack of index cards you stashed.

5. All that's left is the **reveal**. Slowly turn over the index card and collect your reward. Point out that your parent has to honor their promise. They signed it!

YOU CAN EAT ICE CREAM FOR DINNER!

Performance Step 5

SAW A LADY IN HALF

ICE CREAM FOR DINNER works because your parent's brain sees two halves of an object and is fooled into thinking the object is whole. Scientists call this *visual completion*: your brain sees parts of an image and then completes the full picture. Can you think of other examples? What about this dog behind this tree? Is there one? Or maybe two?

In 1921, P. T. Selbit created the famous magic trick Sawing Through a Woman. Take a look: Do you see a similarity here? Is there one woman or two? Hmm, I wonder how this trick works. . . .

COIN SLAM

THE COIN VANISH in this trick is one of the first coin effects I ever learned. But I've added a fun twist so you can go out with a bang! My favorite part of this trick is that you **end clean**. Ending clean means that there's nothing hidden in your hands at the finish. Your nosy parents won't find a thing. You've gotten rid of all the evidence!

THE SECRET

Vanish the coin using a clever method of folding the paper. A secret opening in the paper allows you to steal the coin.

YOU'LL NEED

- A quarter
- A piece of printer paper
- A printer
- A book
- Your magic case

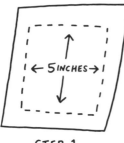

STEP 1

STEP 2

Setup Steps 1 & 2

THE SETUP

1. Take a photo of your quarter or find an image of one online. Make it just a bit smaller than a real quarter and print it in the middle of a piece of printer paper.

2. Then cut the paper so that it's about five inches square, with the image of the quarter still in the middle.

PERFORMANCE

1. Ask your parent for a quarter or use your own. Then bring out the piece of paper but keep the side with the printed coin toward you. If you like, you can carefully place the coin on the piece of paper, directly on top of the printed coin. Because the image is slightly smaller, the real coin will cover it completely. Now you're free to show both sides of the paper as long as you hold the coin in place.

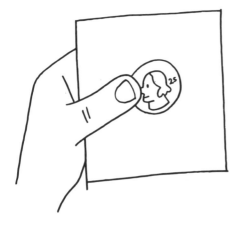

Performance Step 1

2. Keeping the coin side toward you, fold up the bottom half so that its edge comes up to just within an inch of the top edge (a). Then fold the right side over the left side, with the crease about a quarter inch from the coin (b). After this, fold the left side behind so that the paper wraps around the coin (c).

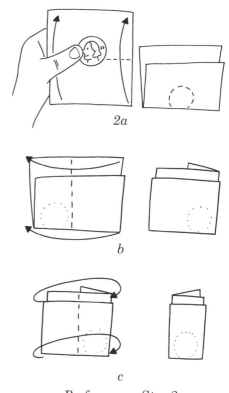

2a

b

c

Performance Step 2

3. This next step is the trickiest: before folding, you need to slide the coin closer to the opening of the packet. The easiest way to do this is to turn everything upside down so the coin falls closer to the opening—but don't let it slip out! Place your fingers there as a stopper. Now you can fold the entire packet in half, so you have a tight paper packet around the coin—or at least that's what it seems like!

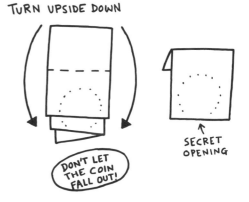

TURN UPSIDE DOWN

DON'T LET THE COIN FALL OUT!

SECRET OPENING

Performance Step 3

Performance Step 4

4. In a moment you are going to **steal** the coin with your right hand. But first, show your parent both sides of the paper packet. Let them tap the paper to feel that the coin is still in there. Then, holding the packet at your fingertips, allow the coin to slide into your hand. You can easily make a fist around the coin while still holding the packet.

5. Take the packet into your left hand. At the same time, your right hand, with the coin, goes to get a big book from your **magician's case** and **ditches** the coin in the process. Picking up the book is the **misdirection** for this move. It gives your parent a false reason for why you went to your case. How sneaky!

6. Place the packet of paper on the table and SLAM! drop the heavy book on the packet. Slide everything toward your parent and have them unfold the paper to find the coin is now two-dimensional. You know what else is flattened? Your parent's sense of the laws of physics!

7. Your parent will look for the real coin, but the evidence is gone. By ditching it before, you've ended clean.

Performance Step 6

T. NELSON DOWNS (1867–1938)

IMAGINE A MAGICIAN reaching up and plucking a shiny coin out of thin air. He tosses it into a bucket—*Clink*. He does it again. *Clink*. And again and again and again. *Clink, clink, clink!* He produces dozens and dozens of coins, entire fistfuls of them, the coins shimmering and cascading noisily into the bucket. This mesmerizing routine was called The Miser's Dream, and it was the signature trick of T. Nelson Downs. Downs was one of the greatest coin manipulators to have ever lived. Manipulation is the branch of magic that involves sleight of hand on stage. It's the art of skillfully making objects like cards and coins appear, disappear, and multiply. Downs was so accomplished at coin manipulation that he went by the title "The King of Koins."

Trick 3

FANCY FOOTWORK

IN MY MAGIC and puzzle show, *The Enigmatist*, one of my favorite effects is called a multiple selection card trick. You've heard of "Pick a card, any card?" This is "Pick ten cards, any ten cards!" After mixing the selections back in the deck, I find all the cards using fancy shuffles and cuts that cause them to spring into my hand or spin through the air.

But sometimes I get one of the cards wrong. That's right, even the professionals make mistakes. The most important thing is never to panic. I calmly ask the audience member what card they actually chose, and with a wave of my hand, I change the wrong card into the correct one. Everyone thinks I missed the card on purpose to set up for this transformation!

This is called having an **out**, a backup plan for when something gets screwed up. You just learned Coin Slam, but what do you do if you ever drop the coin on the floor? I'm going to teach you an out that involves vanishing the coin. Master this and your parents will never know that something went wrong.

THE SECRET
You shoot the coin under your foot.

YOU'LL NEED
• A coin

Performance Step 1

THE SETUP

No setup needed. This is your backup plan for when you drop a coin.

PERFORMANCE

1. If you ever drop the coin on the floor, try this vanish: As you approach the coin to pick it up, plant one of your feet a few inches away from the coin. Then, as you stoop to pick up the coin, shoot it underneath your foot. Make sure to slide the coin

in the same motion as you pretend to come up with the coin.

2. Pretend to hold the coin in your hand and toss it into the air. Look upward in surprise as it doesn't come down again.

3. You can vanish the coin entirely or you can reveal it under your shoe and play the whole trick as a joke. Either way, this out enables you to stay in control of your show. Your parent might even think you meant to drop the coin. You just performed a real, professional out!

Performance Step 2

MAKE THE TRICK BETTER

If you have a second coin, you can turn this out into a cool teleportation effect.

PERFORMANCE

1. Have a backup coin in your pocket. After you shoot the first coin under your foot and vanish it, reveal that the coin has traveled to your pocket by taking out the second one.

2. Next, explain that you are going to have the coin travel impossibly through your body. Place the second coin back in your pocket. With your other hand, use your finger to point out that the coin is now moving up your arm. Squirm and shake a little as the coin travels through your body. Trace the path of the coin as it goes across your chest, down your other arm, all the way through your leg, and out of your foot onto the floor. Show everyone the first coin and you're done.

Performance Step 2

This trick is so fun to perform, sometimes I drop the coin on purpose to set up for this effect.

PHONY PHONE

YOU'VE HEARD IT over and over again from your parents: "Put your cell phone away!" Okay, fine. . . . And just like that, you vanish your cell phone into nothingness! Did you use the sorcery of the Druidic clerics? The wizardry of the Norse gods? Nope, it was a variation on a classic stage illusion, plus something magicians call **time misdirection**. This is a technique for warping when your audience thinks the trick happens. With these powerful tools, you can make almost anything disappear into thin air.

THE SECRET

A little bit of cardboard is all you need to keep the shape of the phone after you've ditched it.

YOU'LL NEED

- A cell phone
- Scissors
- A cloth napkin
- Removable invisible tape
- Some cardboard

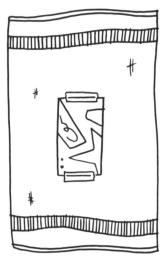

Setup Step 1

Setup Step 2

THE SETUP

You're going to make a cardboard "shell" of your cell phone.

1. Find a piece of thin cardboard—thin enough that you can crumple it up. You'll see why! (A side of a cereal box is perfect for this.) Next, trace an outline of your cell phone and cut it out.

2. Take that piece of cardboard and tape it to a cloth napkin. Use as much tape as you need to get the cardboard to stick, but make sure you're using removable tape. Gently fold the napkin around the cardboard and place it on the table or put it on your case.

PERFORMANCE

1. Hold up your cell phone and put it on the table. Say to your parent, "I know I've been spending too much time on my phone. So, I have a solution for that. . . ."

Performance Step 2

2. Hold up the cloth napkin by the corners, keeping the cardboard side toward you.

3. Place the napkin on top of your phone, lining up the cardboard piece with your phone's edges.

Performance Step 3

4. Curl your fingers around everything and slide the phone toward you so that it clears the edge of the table. Release your grip slightly to **ditch** the phone by letting it fall onto your lap. While you're talking to your parent, find a moment to sit on your phone or slip it into your pocket.

Performance Step 4

5. Continue to hold the cardboard, allowing the cloth napkin to hang down and maintain the shape of

Performance Step 5

Performance Step 6

the phone. Use a full grip around this "shell" of your phone, as if you are still holding it. Everyone will believe it is there. They have no reason not to. But the trick is over before the audience thinks it has even started!

⑥. Hold up the "phone" nice and high. Even better, lean forward so the phone is far away from the edge of the table. Start talking to your parent again: "Remember how you said you wanted me to get rid of my phone? Let me show you something cool. . . ." This is time misdirection. It distances you from where and when the trick actually happened. The longer you talk while holding the phone shell high above the table, the more your parent will forget that you slid the napkin toward the table's edge. Ask your parent to join you in saying some magic words. "Abracadabra!" "Sim Sala Bim!" "Oodles of noodles!" The more fun you have with this and the longer it takes, the more time misdirection you are using.

7. Remember, your parent still thinks nothing has happened yet! After you've cast your spell, crumple the napkin into a small ball and throw it over your shoulder. Your phone is gone!

Performance Step 7

TALMA (1861–1944)

TALMA WAS AN English magician who billed herself as "The Queen of Coins" for her accomplished sleight of hand work. She was best known for being part of the act "Le Roy, Talma & Bosco." In 1914 in London, Talma and Servais Le Roy (her husband) debuted a brand-new illusion called Asrah the Floating Princess. Talma lay on a couch and Le Roy covered her with a cloth. The cloth floated up and up—the audience could still see the shape of Talma's body in the cloth—and suddenly, she was gone! Does this sound familiar? The big illusions are simply larger variations of the small tricks!

COLORFUL CONJURING

WITH THIS STUNNING demonstration of conjuring, you are going to vanish multiple objects at once. Vanishing one crayon is cool. Vanishing a bunch of them at the same time is impossible! You're going to first show your parents normal crayons and then **switch** them out for **gimmicked** ones. Colorful Conjuring is a remarkable visual illusion that will cause your parents' jaws to land on the floor. I still fool my friends and family with it all the time!

THE SECRET
You've rigged the box of crayons.

YOU'LL NEED
- A box of crayons (a pack of eight is best)
- Scissors
- Thick tape
- A playing card

Setup Step 1

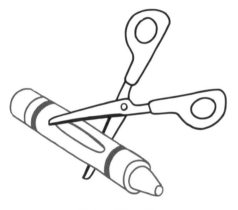

Setup Step 2

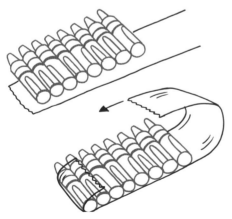

Setup Step 3

THE SETUP

1. To create your gimmicked crayon box, start by emptying the crayons from the box. Many crayon boxes come with an illustrated window. If the box already has a real window, then you're all set. If not, use a pair of scissors to carefully cut out a window to match the illustrated one.

2. Next, take all the crayons and use scissors to cut them in half. Be sure to be as precise as possible so that all your crayons are the same size.

3. Tape all of your crayon halves together. It's easiest if you lay out a piece of tape and line up all the crayons on top of it. Wrap the tape around the crayons to secure them and cut off any excess tape.

4. Put your crayon halves back in the box and turn it upside down so the crayons slide toward the top. If you squeeze on the box, the crayons will stay in place, visible through the window. If you release the pressure, they will fall down out of sight. Cool right? Bring the crayons back into view and you're ready to go!

PERFORMANCE

1. This effect is best done when following a trick that uses real crayons like Crayon Clairvoyance (p. 113). After you've performed that trick, take the box of crayons back from your parent and place it in your magician's case for just a moment—just long enough to switch it for the gimmicked box of crayons. Set that on the table. Want to use more time misdirection? Do an entirely different trick and come back to the crayons on the table later. Some of

Setup Step 4

the sneakiest magic moves happen *in between* tricks!

2. When you're ready to perform the effect, grab the crayons and hold the box tightly so the crayons stay in place. With your other hand, pick up the playing card and momentarily block the window. When you relax your grip, the crayons fall below the window. But the playing card acts as cover, so your parents can't see any motion.

Performance Step 2

Timing is everything! If you can release the crayons at the exact second the card obscures them, you can vanish them instantaneously. I like to move the card in a circular motion to make it seem like I am magically rubbing the crayons away.

DOUG HENNING (1947–2000)

THERE WAS NO more colorful magician than Doug Henning. In his joyful performances, Henning wore bright, sparkly costumes that featured rainbows, stars, and moons. Henning rose to fame while starring in *The Magic Show*, a Broadway musical, in 1974. But Henning was just getting started. In 1975, he became the first great television magician, airing *Doug Henning's World of Magic* live to over 50 million people.

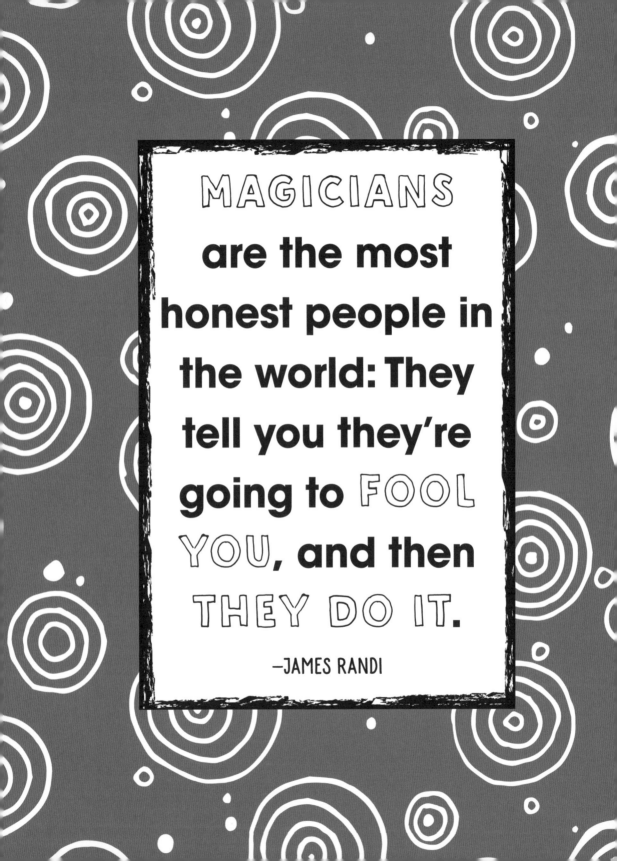

MAGICIANS are the most honest people in the world: They tell you they're going to FOOL YOU, and then THEY DO IT.

—JAMES RANDI

THE GREAT COOKIE CAPER

YOU ARE ABOUT TO perform the most delicious magic trick of all time. Your parent will choose a playing card and it will magically end up inside a chocolate chip cookie!

This trick will use one of the most important principles in magic: the **force**. Move over, Luke Skywalker, you are going to *make* your parent choose a playing card! Of course, they will believe they have selected the card freely. That's the most essential element to preserve—that everything is fair (it's not!).

Once you have learned how to force a card, there are unlimited possibilities for how you can impossibly **reveal** it. If you force your parent to choose the seven of hearts, for example, you can have a second seven of hearts in your shoe, buried in the backyard, or floating out of a deck in space (it's been done!). On the next page, you'll learn how to reveal it inside the most celebrated of all baked goods: the chocolate chip cookie.

YOU'LL NEED

- A deck of cards
- A duplicate playing card
- Ingredients for your favorite chocolate chip cookie recipe

Setup Step 1

Setup Step 2

THE SETUP

The setup involves baking a card into a cookie. Ask one of your parents to help you with this part. You can fool the other!

1. Grab a duplicate card, like the eight of spades. Fold the card into quarters and crease it so it lies flat.

2. Place it in the middle of the dough and mold around it, covering it completely. Don't worry, the paper won't burn inside the cookie!

PERFORMANCE

Invite your parent to pick a card. But you're going to *force* them to choose the eight of spades. It's important that they think they have a free choice of any card when you are in fact making them choose the eight. Let's use a great force called the Double Cut Force!

DOUBLE CUT FORCE
(see diagram on next page)

1. Start with the eight of spades secretly on the top of the deck. Hand the deck to your parent and have them cut about a third of the cards and flip them over on the deck itself. If needed, you can demonstrate how to do this; just make sure you put the eight of spades back on top. Next, tell them to cut even more, around two-thirds, and flip that over on the deck again. The deck is now in the following condition: a run of faceup cards on top of facedown cards, the first of which is the original top card, the eight of spades.

2. Say to your parent: "Now that you've marked where your cut is, spread through the cards. Take the first facedown card and look at it but don't show me."

3. While they are looking at their card, take the deck back and straighten out all the cards. Then return their card to the middle of the deck, losing it.

DOUBLE CUT FORCE

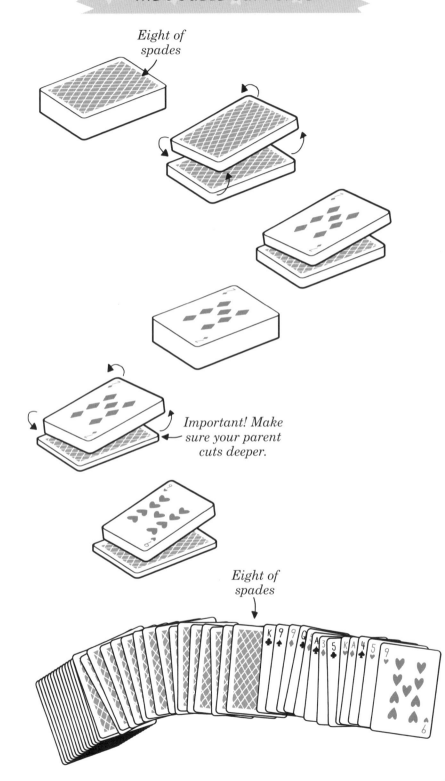

Eight of spades

Important! Make sure your parent cuts deeper.

Eight of spades

4. Next, bring out a plate of freshly baked cookies and ask your parent, "Wouldn't it be amazing if your card vanished from the deck and ended up inside one of these delicious cookies?" Remember, performance is everything. Sell the idea that the eight of spades is traveling invisibly from the cards to the cookies. Maybe you wave the deck over the cookies. Or pretend to grab an invisible card and throw it toward the plate. Be creative with your story!

Performance Step 4

5. Hand your parent the cookie with the eight of spades in it and have them break it open. Inside will be a folded-up scrumptious miracle!

6. The perfect time to find the original eight of spades and slip

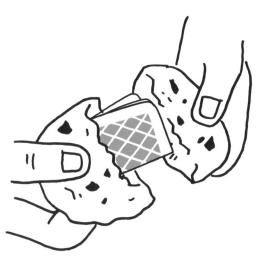

Performance Step 5

it into your pocket is while your parent opens the cookie. Also, you don't have to show them that the card is no longer in the deck. It's better to leave the deck on the table and walk away. Your snooping parent will go looking for it when you've left the room. They might think they are onto you, but you're always a step ahead!

MAKE THE TRICK
BETTER

Just before the cookies finish baking, while the dough is still slightly soft, have your parent help you position chocolate chips in the shape of an "8" on the cookie with the card in it. After the cookie cools, place several more chips on the top of it so that the 8 is not obvious. Before breaking the cookie open, give the cookie a magical shake so the extra chips fall off it. The 8 will materialize into view!

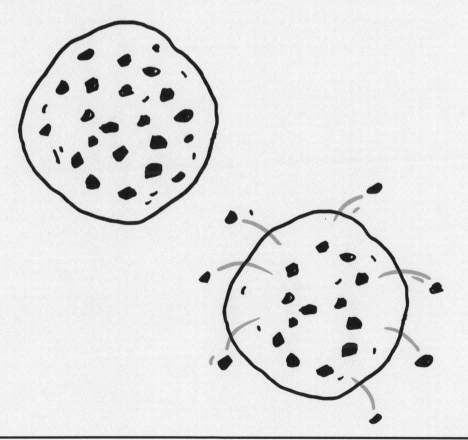

AL BAKER (1874–1951)

INSPIRED TO DO more baking tricks? One of the greatest comedy effects in magic was Cake Baked in a Hat by Al Baker. Baker's signature routine involved borrowing a hat from the audience and cracking eggs into it. After combining other ingredients in the hat, he would produce a real sponge cake. Baker would not only return the hat undamaged, he would also cut up the cake and serve it to the audience for a tasty treat!

ROYAL FLUSH

NEXT, I'M GOING to teach you an astonishing teleportation. You tear the corner off a card and flush the rest of the card down the toilet. And voilà! The card reappears in an envelope and the corner matches. In this trick you'll learn a switch that professional magicians use. It's sneaky, deceptive, and is guaranteed to confound your parents.

THE SECRET

Using a diabolical corner switch, you can impossibly make the corners match.

YOU'LL NEED

- A duplicate playing card
- An envelope
- A pen

Setup Step 1

THE SETUP

A duplicate playing card. Let's say it's the three of hearts.

1. Tear the corner off the card (the one with the number three on it) and put it in your pocket. Let's call this corner (A).

2. Take the rest of card (A) and seal it in an envelope that you've written "prediction" on.

PERFORMANCE

1. Point out the prediction envelope and leave it on the table. Make a big deal about how you will go nowhere near it.

2. Have your parent take a "random" playing card, the three of hearts (B). If you hand it to them casually, it will seem spontaneous. Or use the Double Cut

Force to make them pick the three of hearts.

3. Tear off the corner of the three of hearts (B) in the same place you did it with the duplicate card. It won't be an exact match, but try to come as close as possible. I promise, your parent will never notice the difference!

Performance Step 3

4. Hold it up, saying, "This is like your receipt. The proof that this is your card. I want you to keep it safe in your pocket, like this. . . ." Demonstrate in your own pocket where they should put it. But this is when you switch the corner for the duplicate corner you already have! Bring out corner (A) and hand it to your parent to place in their pocket.

Performance Step 4

5. Next, you must completely dispose of your parent's three of hearts (B).

Bring your parent into the bathroom, rip the card into small pieces, and flush those down the toilet. Make sure those pieces are small! Down the toilet is perfect because there has to be no way for your parent to see card (B) again.

Performance Step 5

⑤。 Turn your attention to the envelope and have your parent open it. Have them remove the predicted card (A). It's the three of hearts! And for the big moment, have them take corner (A) from their pocket and match it perfectly. A true miracle!

Performance Step 6

One way to enhance your prediction is to send it through the mail. Address the envelope to your parent and write on the back, "Do not open until magic show!"

RENÉ LAVAND (1928–2015)

SLEIGHT OF HAND doesn't have to be fast. If you have strong misdirection, you can control where your audience looks and what they believe. René Lavand was born Héctor Renato Lavandera in Buenos Aires, Argentina. When he was nine years old, he lost his right hand in a car crash. But this did not stop Lavand from becoming an international name in magic. His catchphrase was "No se puede hacer más lento," Spanish for "It cannot be done any slower." Performing his signature card trick at slow pace, Lavand would challenge his audience to catch him in the act. He would mix the suit colors, red and black, and somehow instantly separate the colors again. His audience never stood a chance.

PART TWO

TECHNOLOGICAL TRICKERY

DIGITAL
DECEPTION

THERE'S AN INDISPUTABLE fact that has been true since the beginning of civilization. It's a law of humankind that has puzzled historians and sociologists for centuries: parents are slow to adopt technology. Exhibit A: my parents still have their landline and an answering machine!

And you know who's the best with embracing the latest tech developments? Magicians. Conjurers have harnessed electromagnetism, holograms, and microcircuitry to pull off their impossible feats.

What a perfect combination! You are poised to fool the heck out of your parents with the tricks in this chapter. On the following pages, I've selected for you a number of effects that use today's technology—tricks with cell phones, cameras, and AI. And with the popularity of Zoom and FaceTime, I'll show you how to perform miracles that take advantage of video calls.

Your parents don't always understand today's technology. Now, imagine combining the digital wizardry of your devices with a little sleight of hand to create the ultimate confusion!

CRYPTOCURRENCY

IT'S A LOT of fun to take a digital image and transform it into a real object. In this trick I'll teach you a coin effect that does just that! What makes this illusion even more deceptive is you can let your parents pick which coin they want you to materialize. Well, they don't *really* get to decide—you're going to use a forcing technique called **magician's choice**. After you master this, your parents will never have free choice again. Remember to use your new powers for good, not evil!

THE SECRET

By hiding a coin beneath the phone, you can magically make it appear.

YOU'LL NEED

- A smartphone

- A penny, a nickel, and a quarter. Only the nickel will be used in the performance.

THE SETUP

On a neutral background like an empty table, take these two photos in this order:

ⓐ. A penny and a quarter in a line. Leave an empty space between them where a nickel is supposed to be.

ⓑ. Now add the nickel. You have three coins in a row: the penny, the nickel, and the quarter.

This setup and the instructions below are for producing the coin with your right hand. If you want to use your left hand, switch the order of the photos.

Steps a & b

PERFORMANCE

1. Start with the nickel hidden under the phone in your left hand, your fingertips pressing it against the phone case.

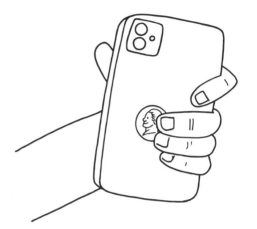

Performance Step 1

2. As you introduce the trick and gesture to your parent, you can easily switch the hand that holds the phone and nickel. As your right hand takes the phone, your right fingers take the place of the left fingers—the coin never moves.

You can do this exchange as many times as you like, and it will reinforce the idea that you are not concealing anything.

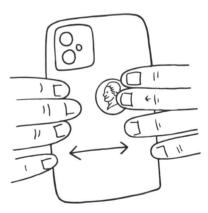
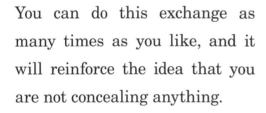

Performance Step 2

3. Ask your parent if they have heard of digital currency. Point to your phone and say, "In fact, I have some digital currency right here." Show them the photo of the three coins.

4. You are now going to use magician's choice. Secretly, you will ensure that your parent chooses the nickel, the coin you have under the phone. Say to your parent: "Imagine that you are removing two coins from the phone. Go ahead, invisibly grab them. Which ones are they?"

If they say the penny and the quarter, then you're set! Say, "Wonderful, you've left me with the nickel," which will be the coin you will produce in a moment. This is the best outcome and happens frequently.

But if your parent chooses to invisibly grab the penny and the nickel, you say, "Great, now please hand one back to me." If they pretend to hand you the nickel, say, "Wonderful, you've chosen to use the nickel for this trick." If they hand you the penny, you say, "Fabulous, you've decided to keep the nickel for this trick."

Use the same bit of choice manipulation if they invisibly grab the quarter and the nickel. The important thing to remember is you are affirming *their choice* to use the nickel. In magic, you never want to tell your audience what the end of the trick will be. This way, you can always pivot the story to make things work in your favor.

5. Now the fun part: producing the nickel. If your right hand is doing the move, get ready by having the coin on the fingertips of the same hand underneath the phone. Use your left hand to stabilize the phone by grabbing it on the left side. As your right hand slides the coin out from underneath the phone, your right thumb drags across the screen, swiping right to the previous photo. This is the photo that shows the nickel missing, of course. If you do all of this in one quick motion, it will seem like you are pulling the coin out of the screen! And it's the coin they chose!

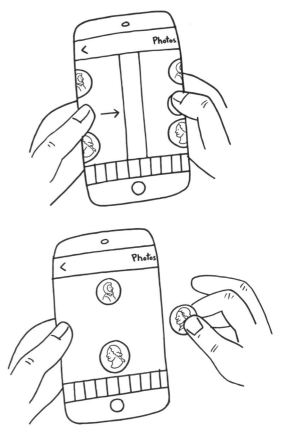

Performance Step 5

JEAN-EUGÈNE ROBERT-HOUDIN
(1805–1871)

MANY PEOPLE CONSIDER Jean-Eugène Robert-Houdin to be the founding father of magic. He was so influential that Harry Houdini chose to name himself after him. Robert-Houdin was a brilliant adopter of technology. One of his most famous tricks was called the Light and Heavy Chest. Robert-Houdin would introduce a small wooden box with a metal handle. He would invite a child to join him onstage and lift up the box with ease. Then he would ask an adult, usually a strong man, to try to lift the box. The man would strain and strain and be unable to budge the box even an inch. The secret? Robert-Houdin had hidden an electromagnet beneath the stage. When he turned it on, the magnetic force exerted on the metal handle made the box unmovable!

SCREEN SORCERY

MAGIC IS ABOUT controlling what your audience can and can't see. When you're doing magic through a camera, you can take advantage of the fact that your audience has to look straight ahead at you. They watch the trick through what magicians call the **frame**. And for tricks done over video, many secret moves happen "outside the frame." For example, you could have a friend sitting next to you, secretly handing you objects, and your audience would never know!

On the next page, I'll teach you a mind-blowing trick that you can do through the camera. It's the perfect effect for fooling a family member over Zoom, FaceTime, etc.

THE SETUP

1. Write "PREDICTION" in big bold letters on an index card.

2. Next, write the names of all the United States presidents on separate index cards. On the back side, write "PREDICTION" in the exact same way as you did before. It will take you a few minutes, but this extra preparation is what makes the trick work!

3. Place the index cards in alphabetical order neatly in front of you, but off to the side, outside the camera's frame.

Setup Step 3

PERFORMANCE

1. Display the prediction index card for all to see. Mention that you are going to leave this card in plain view the entire time.

Performance Step 1

2. Hold the index card with your left hand and slowly move the index card to the bottom right corner of the screen. Note: on your parent's screen, this will appear in the *lower left* corner of your parent's view of you, like in the image to the right. Do this casually, but positioning is key! The most important thing is that the bottom and right sides of the card are *out of frame*.

Performance Step 2

3. Next, ask your parent to name any president of the United States. Any one, free choice! Perhaps they choose

Performance Step 3

Performance Step 4

Performance Step 5

Kennedy. Secretly glance down at the rows of index cards that are off-camera and with your right hand steal the Kennedy card.

4. While keeping your prediction card absolutely still, **load** the Kennedy card behind it. Because the bottom and right sides of the prediction card are out of frame, you can slide the Kennedy card behind it undetected. It helps if you lay your index fingers on the top edge of the prediction card so that they act as a stopper, keeping the two cards aligned.

5. Once the two cards are flush together, bring them into the middle of the screen. Use both hands to keep them aligned. Carefully turn the two cards over together to reveal that you predicted Kennedy correctly.

6. While your parent is freaking out, lower the two cards to the bottom of the screen so that the bottom edge of the cards dip just out of sight. Release the prediction card, ditching it out of frame, so that you're holding just the Kennedy card. Casually, show that PREDICTION is written on the reverse side. Once again, you've ended clean!

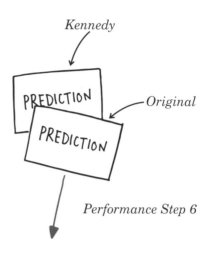

Kennedy

Original

Performance Step 6

MAKE THE TRICK
BETTER

It can't hurt to write the name of a president on the other side of your prediction card. Every once in a while, the president that your parent (or other audience member) chooses will be the one you're already holding. You'll have a miracle on your hands! What president do you think people will choose most often? Is it Abraham Lincoln? Teddy Roosevelt? Probably not Millard Fillmore, but hey, you never know!

GEORGES MÉLIÈS
(1861–1938)

DID YOU KNOW that movies grew out of magic? The first film director, Frenchman Georges Méliès, started as a magician. In 1888, he purchased Robert-Houdin's magical theater and developed dozens of brand-new illusions. With an early camera, Méliès filmed many of these tricks, creating some of the first movies. One of his first films, *The Vanishing Lady*, shows Méliès covering a woman with a cloth and making her disappear. Sound familiar? Directors control the frame of where you look and what you experience. It's all magic.

HEY, MINERVA

THIS NEXT TRICK is an effect with Artificial Intelligence, or at least that's what you'll convince your parent is happening.

One of the most well-guarded secrets in magic is that the assistant often does the real work. For example, say the magician has just produced a rabbit. When the assistant comes onstage to remove the rabbit, they are sneaking the magician a dove for the next trick.

For this illusion, you will be the assistant. It's best to pretend you have nothing to do with the AI mind reading at HeyMinerva .com. But, of course, you are pulling the strings the entire time! Minerva was a real magician who performed in the early 1900s. She took her name from the Roman goddess of wisdom.

YOU'LL NEED

- A smartphone or computer

THE SETUP

Practice the secret input method so that you can do it quickly.

PERFORMANCE

1. Tell your parent that over a hundred years ago there was a magician named Minerva and that her spirit lives on in artificial intelligence. Before you visit Minerva, have a casual conversation with your parent about what question they want to ask her. You can suggest to your parent to ask a question that you secretly already know the answer to. If you don't know the answer, casually ask your parent to reveal it. Don't worry, Minerva will be the one performing the magic! Let's say the answer to the question is the name of your parent's first dog, Droolius Caesar.

2. On your phone or computer, visit HeyMinerva.com. You will find a woman with a crystal ball and a text box that reads "Message Minerva."

3. The trickery starts right away. In the text box, your parent sees that you are typing "Hey, Minerva, are you there?" when you are really typing something else.

How? If you start typing with a period (.), you switch into secret input mode. Thanks to some fancy programming, even though you are typing ".Droolius Caesar.," the letters of "Hey, Minerva, are you there?" will appear on the screen.

When you are done inputting the secret answer, hit a period (.) again. You can now finish typing the letters of "Hey, Minerva, are you there?" Then hit the send icon or press Enter. Note that if you ever need to start over, simply refresh the page.

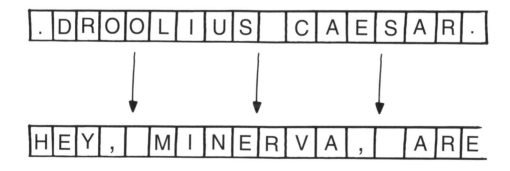

4. Minerva will respond with, "Yes, I am here. Who is in my presence?" You can have your parent type in the response. They can type anything from "It's Dad and Maya" to "This is John." Have your parent press Enter.

The purpose of this step is misdirection. You want your parent to believe that all the typing is real. In magic, we call this the "convincer." You are convincing your parent that everything is fair. But it's not! You already did the tricky part!

5. Minerva will then say, "Please ask me your question." Have your parent type, "What was the name of my first dog?" and then hit Enter. Minerva will think for a few seconds and then reveal, "Droolius Caesar." Remember to look just as surprised as your parent!

MINERVA (???)

MINERVA WAS AN escape artist who was known as "The Queen of Mystery." The exact dates of her life are unknown, but she flourished from 1900–1920. Her real name was most likely Margaretha Gertz Van Dorn. She was a rival of Houdini's because, like so many imitators, she performed his Milk Can Escape. Minerva would be handcuffed and submerged in a wooden barrel that had been dramatically filled to the brim. A curtain would go up and Minerva would somehow free herself from her restraints and the barrel. She was also known for doing bridge jumps. In 1908, in Cumberland, Maryland, Minerva was handcuffed by the chief of police and leapt from the Blue Bridge into the Potomac River. As the crowd nervously watched the murky water, eventually Minerva came to the surface, freed from her shackles!

THE WIZARD 2.0

THIS IS A TELEPHONE trick I used to fool my parents with all the time when I was a kid. It can be done anywhere, anytime. All you need is a **stooge**. A stooge is a secret collaborator. Some of the best illusions rely on stooges. As long as your parents are convinced you are acting alone, you can perform some of the most miraculous tricks!

The Wizard is a classic trick that has stood the test of time. On the following pages, I am going to teach you both the original trick and an improvement that is very deceptive.

THE SECRET

You will call your friend who is in on the trick.

YOU'LL NEED:

- A phone
- A friend to call
- A deck of playing cards

THE SETUP

Have a friend be ready as a stooge. They should be familiar with how the trick works.

PERFORMANCE

1. The trick starts with knowing the identity of a chosen playing card. Spread the cards faceup on the table and have your parent pull one out, leaving it faceup. Tell your parent, "It's okay if I see your card, because I won't be the one finding it." Alternatively, you can add a layer of deception to this trick and use one of the card forces in this book. If you do this, your parent can keep their card a secret. In either case, even though you know the identity of your parent's card, your stooge doesn't have to. You're about to clue them in. Let's say your parent selects the five of clubs.

2. Call your friend and say, "Hello. Is the Wizard there?" This is your friend's cue to start slowly saying the values of the cards: "Ace . . . two . . . three . . . four . . . five . . ." Interrupt them when they say "five" with, "Wizard, can you help me with a magic trick?" Your stooge now knows the card's value is five.

3. Next your friend will say the suits: "Hearts . . . diamonds . . . clubs . . ." You interject again: "Great! Hold on, I want you to

speak to someone." Now your stooge knows the card is the five of clubs.

4. Hand the phone to your parent and the Wizard will reveal, "Your card is the five of clubs." The best part about this trick is that you can call at any time. If your stooge is familiar with the trick, then as soon as they hear "Hello. Is the Wizard there?" they will know what to do!

MAKE THE TRICK
BETTER
THE WIZARD 2.0

In this version of the trick, the Wizard can be on speakerphone the entire time.

PERFORMANCE

1. As before, you can force a card or ask your parent to choose one. If your parent is selecting a card, spread the deck on the table face up. Let's say they choose the ten of diamonds.

2. Next, your job is to find their card's "mate." Every card has a match in the same color, just a different suit. The eight of clubs

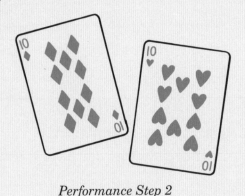

Performance Step 2

pairs with the eight of spades; the queen of hearts pairs with the queen of diamonds. In this case, the mate of the ten of diamonds is the ten of hearts. This time, as you scoop up all the cards, grab the ten of hearts and put it third from the top.

3. You will now spread the cards in a row face down and have your parent place their card anywhere in the deck. Make a big deal about how fair this is. "You can put it back wherever you want!" (Note that you should not let them put it too close to the top because that's where the mate card is. Tell them that would make the trick too easy and encourage them to put it near the middle.)

Mate Card

Performance Step 3

4. When your friend answers the phone, ask for the Wizard and quickly tell them that you'd like to try something on speakerphone.

5. Hand the deck of cards to your parent and ask them to deal the cards face up on the table, saying each card's name as they do so. Tell your stooge that you'd like them to sense telepathically which card your parent chose. But here's the rub! Your stooge knows to listen for the third card, the mate of the chosen card. Once they hear the ten of hearts, they will know that the ten of diamonds is the chosen card. When your parent deals and says the ten of diamonds, your friend will yell, "Stop! That's it!"

Performance Step 5

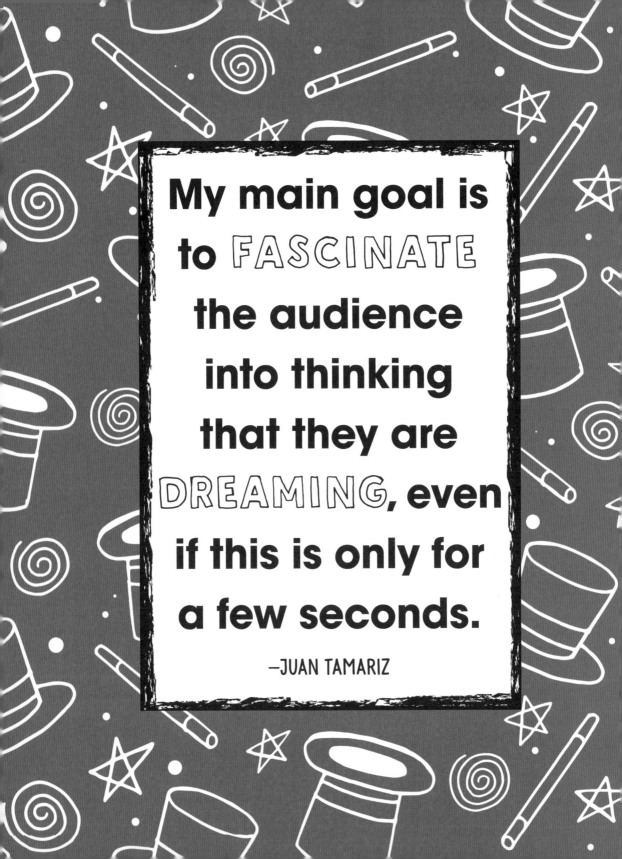

My main goal is to FASCINATE the audience into thinking that they are DREAMING, even if this is only for a few seconds.

—JUAN TAMARIZ

TELEPHONE TELEPATHY

THE WIZARD 2.0 is an amazing trick, but imagine being able to call *any phone number* your parents name. Well, my clever conjurers, I'm about to teach you a truly diabolical technique, one that takes of advantage of today's technology.

Telephone Telepathy is a fabulous tool for having a stranger (your stooge) reveal anything. Try combining it with Wizard 2.0 to reveal a chosen playing card.

THE SECRET

Once again you will call a stooge. But you'll disguise their name in the phone as a stranger's number.

YOU'LL NEED

- A smartphone
- A deck of cards

THE SETUP

Make sure your stooge's number is in the phone already. For Android phones, you might want to create a new contact entry for this person. If they are already in the phone, their photo might show on the screen when you call them. It's best to start with a fresh entry. For iPhones, you don't have to do anything.

PERFORMANCE

1. As in The Wizard 2.0, have your parent choose a card and return it to the deck. Make sure the mate card is secretly third from the top. Place the deck aside for a moment.

2. Take out your cell phone or borrow your parent's. Go to the call screen with the keypad and tell your parent that you are going to call a random number to see if that person can figure out their card. Next, tilt the phone screen toward you so that only you can view it, switch over to the Contacts, and go to your stooge's name. Let's say your friend's name is Francis.

3. Ask your parent to name ten random digits of a phone number. As they do, you pretend to punch them into the keypad. But what you're really doing is editing Francis's contact info: very quickly delete Francis's first and last name. If you are using your parent's phone, make sure you put the name back later!

94

Suppose your parent chooses 202-555-0132. Type that into the field for the first name. You might have to ask them to repeat it, which is fine. Hit DONE so the contact is saved.

4. Call your stooge's real number and put the phone on speaker. Show your parent the call screen. Instead of the usual "Calling Francis," it will say "Calling 202-555-0132." Devious, right?!

5. Note that on Android phones the actual phone number you are calling is shown in small numbers below the fake number. No problem, there's a fix for that on the next page. But I promise you, if you show the call screen very quickly to your parent, they are not going to notice it. This is called **selective attention**. They are not looking for it, so their eyes will only focus on the big numbers.

For example, did you notice that step number 4 on the previous page was in a different font? Nope! That's selective attention.

But here's your fix: After showing the call screen for a few seconds, switch over to the home screen. This will hide the call screen while you keep the call going.

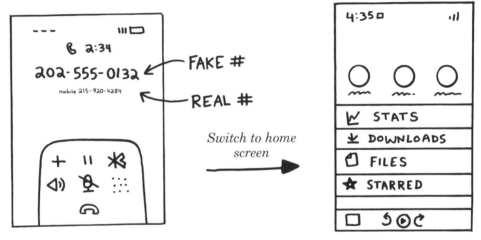

Performance Step 5

6. When your stooge answers the phone, say something like, "Hi. This is David calling. I know this is totally weird, but I'm a magician and I'm doing a magic trick right now. Can you help me with something? What's your name?" Your friend should pretend to be surprised or maybe even a bit annoyed that you are interrupting their day. You too should act spontaneously:

"Thank you for your help, Frankie. Sorry, what's your name again? Oh, right, it's Francis."

7. You're now set up to finish The Wizard 2.0. Your parent will deal the cards and a total stranger will know what card they chose.

8. Pick up the phone and hold the screen toward you. Thank Frankie . . . er, Francis for their time. After the trick, if you borrowed your parent's phone and added your stooge into their contacts, make sure you delete the whole contact. If you're using your own phone, simply put their name back to how it was before.

CHING LING FOO (1854–1922)

CHING LING FOO was the first magician from Asia to achieve global fame. In 1898, Foo toured the United States and sparked a craze for Chinese magic. His signature feat was producing a huge porcelain bowl, brimming with water, from an empty silk shawl. Foo was also known for pulling colored ribbons from his mouth and spurting flames. But a favorite effect of Foo's was a simple restoration, and one of the first of its kind: Foo's paper-tearing trick.

Displaying that his hands were empty, Foo would rip a strip of paper into small pieces. He did this in a slow and fair manner so the audience could watch his every movement. To finish, Foo brought his hands together and pulled out the paper strip in one piece, whole again. Foo would perform this trick several times in succession, with both audiences and fellow magicians unable to detect his secrets.

A FORCE FROM ANYWHERE!

IN THIS NEXT TRICK, I am going to teach you a neat card force that you can do from anywhere. That's because it works over Zoom, FaceTime, etc.

As you've learned in this book, the secrets of magic tricks are often very simple. But it's your job as a magician to enhance the magical moment. The best way to do this is to create opportunities that allow your parents' imaginations to run wild. In other words, you want your parents to *overthink* things.

This trick hinges on forcing a card on your parents. But then you are going to *sell* it as something else. Exactly what? That's for them to imagine. . . .

THE SECRET

The Cross Cut Force. One of the *best* forces in all of magic. I should really make you take the magician's oath again before I teach you this one.

YOU'LL NEED

• A computer or smartphone with Zoom, FaceTime, etc.

• A deck of cards that your parent provides

THE SETUP

For your parent on the other end of the video call, there is no setup. Just have them bring a deck of playing cards.

PERFORMANCE

1. Hop on a Zoom or FaceTime call with your parent and tell them they'll need a deck of cards. Start by asking them to take the cards out of the box and shuffle them really well.

2. When they've finished, say, "Let's make sure they are really mixed. Can you hold them up and spread them in front of the camera? Great! Nice job." You are giving them a false reason for why you want them to hold up the cards. The real reason is that this action allows you to look at the bottom card of their deck and

Performance Step 2

remember it. Misdirection is not always about controlling where your audience is looking. Often, it's about controlling what they're *thinking*.

3. Tell your parent to square up the cards and place them on the table facedown. Ask them to tilt their camera down so you can see the cards. You know the bottom card of the deck. Let's say it's the ace of spades. Now you'll force them to choose it.

Cross Cut Force: Have your parent cut the cards roughly in half by putting the top half on the table next to the bottom half. Then ask them to take the bottom half and place it on the top half at a 45-degree angle.

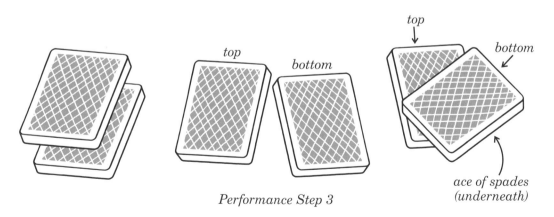

CROSS CUT FORCE

Performance Step 3

ace of spades (underneath)

Next is the most important part: talk to your parent for about eight seconds. Distract them! Talk about the weather, music, how cotton candy was invented by a dentist (it's true). Probably the best thing to mention is how they just cut the cards freely wherever they wanted. It's your old friend, time misdirection! You are putting some space between what just happened and what you want them to remember. In other words, you're getting them to forget which half of the deck was which.

You can now go back to the cards. Say the following to your parent: "Please lift up the top half of the deck and turn it toward you so you can see the card that you cut to. Don't show it to me!" Note two things: 1) You are calling it the "top half" (it's not!). 2) Don't say "look at the 'bottom card,'" as that might remind them which half the card actually came from. "The card that you cut to" (they didn't!) is much better.

♧. As with so many of these tricks, the hard part is over. You can choose to reveal the ace of spades in any manner you like. But I like the following way, as it plays with technology and really messes with their minds.

Ask them to remove their card and keep it hidden. In a moment, you're going to have them hold up the face of the card to the camera, but first they're going to *turn it off.*

You, on the other hand, will keep your camera on so your parent can watch you telepathically sensing their card. Say something like, "I'm getting a feeling. . . . It's a black card, right? . . . It's a club . . . no, wait, it's a spade! . . . It's a high spade. . . . Yes, I think I have it!"

Performance Step 4

But don't reveal the card just yet. The fun of magic is seeing the exact moment your audience member's jaw drops. Ask your parent to put their card face down on the table and turn the camera back on. Now, tell them triumphantly that their card is the ace of spades and soak up the bewildered look on their face.

IT'S ESSENTIAL TO keep your parents out of this book. These professional secrets are too valuable! The following two pages contain some fake math homework. Try leaving this book open to the homework to throw your parents off the scent! Or, if your parents get nosy while you're practicing, you can quickly flip to these pages. See, math homework *can* be fun!

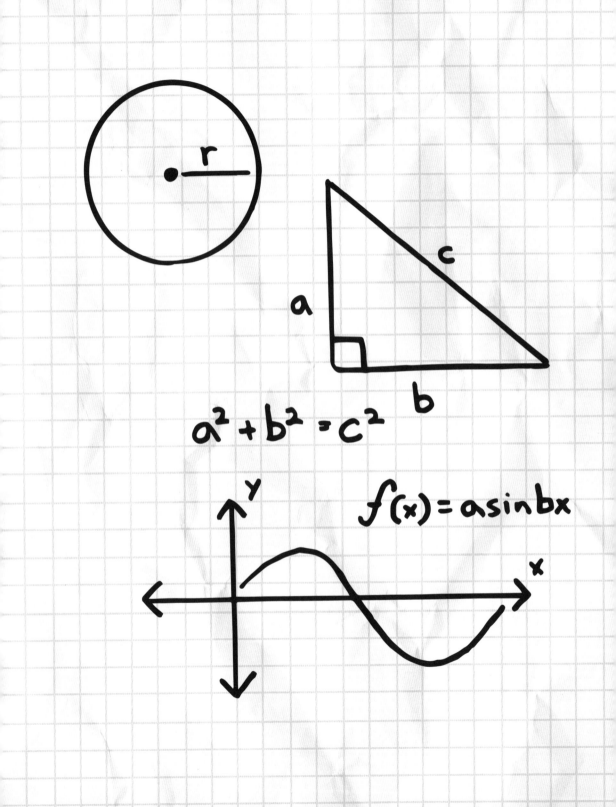

$$a^2 + b^2 = c^2$$

$$f(x) = a \sin bx$$

$$(ab)^n = a^n b^n$$

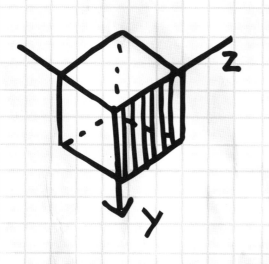

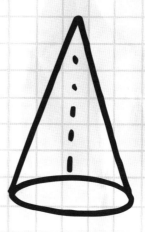

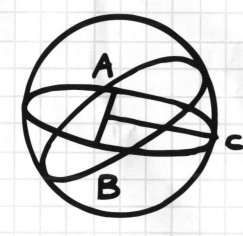

$$a^{\div} = \sqrt[\sim]{a}$$

$$ax^2 + bx + c = 0$$

PART THREE

MENTALISM

MIND OVER MATTER

GET EXCITED TO tell fortunes, read minds, and communicate with the astral plane! Mentalism encompasses any trick that demonstrates the power of one's thoughts. It involves contacting spirits with psychic readings, bending spoons with telekinesis, or predicting lottery numbers with your second sight.

There's no branch of illusion that is more impactful than mentalism. It is magic that is eerie, strange, and leaves your audience wondering for days what happened.

In this chapter, I'll teach you a number of different ways to befuddle your parents with your supernatural mental abilities. You'll learn tricks involving telepathy (reading your parents' thoughts), precognition (knowing their futures), and clairvoyance (using extra-sensory perception, or ESP) to name a few.

If you can get your parents to believe you are a real-life mystic, they might think twice the next time they ask you to clean your room. You can tell them, "Sorry, I'm too busy reading . . . the future with my mind's eye!"

CRAYON CLAIRVOYANCE

HOW MANY SENSES does the average human being have? Five. But you're no average human being! You have extra-sensory perception, or ESP. Your "sixth sense" is clairvoyance, the ability to visualize things with your mind.

Clairvoyance is the power of "clear seeing." You will be able to perceive anything, even if your back is turned, your eyes are closed, or your parents are merely thinking of a word. Get ready to floor your parents with your psychic gifts!

THE SECRET
Use your fingernail to scratch off a bit of colored wax. You'll sneak a peek and convince your parents you have psychic intuition.

YOU'LL NEED
• A box of crayons

THE SETUP

No setup needed! This is a great **impromptu** effect that you can do with any box of crayons.

PERFORMANCE

1. Bring out a box of crayons and tell your parent that every color has its own energy. Maybe you describe how reds have warm energy and blues have cold. And you can sense each color without looking.

2. Turn your back to your parent and have them choose one crayon. Extend your hand behind you and have them give you their selection. Then turn back around, facing your parent while keeping the crayon held behind your back. Make a big deal about how you are trying to feel for the crayon's energy.

3. While you're doing this, secretly scrape your thumb against the crayon, so that a small bit of wax goes under your fingernail. Then, while looking away, have your parent take back the crayon and return it to the box.

Performance Step 3

4. All you need to do now is glance at your nail to know what color was chosen. You can do this casually, or try holding your hands up to "sense the energy all around us." The fingernail with the wax will be right in front of your face!

Performance Step 4

This is a great trick to perform again and again. Just use a different fingernail each time!

MAKE THE TRICK
BETTER

After you've performed Crayon Clairvoyance, return the crayons to the box and switch them for the gimmicked crayons in Colorful Conjuring. Because your parents will have already examined the real crayons, they will be doubly fooled when they disappear!

LULU, THE GEORGIA WONDER
(1869–1950)

AT THE AGE of fourteen, Lulu Hurst was struck by lightning during a mythical electrical storm . . . or so her publicity maintained. After that, sparks would shoot from her hands. In her presence, umbrellas would spring open. Objects would fly around the room. She had become possessed with what she called "The Power" or "The Great Unknown." It was a good story and America gobbled it up. She began calling herself "The Georgia Wonder" or "The Magnetic Girl" and toured the United States from 1884–1885, becoming one of the most famous women in the country. Her act consisted of feats of supernatural strength. For example, Hurst would hold a pole horizontally, and though three burly men would hurl their strength at the pole, she wouldn't budge an inch. Another act involved her "animal magnetism." She would present a cane and challenge any man to take it from her. They failed every time. In reality, Hurst was a master of leverage and force deflection. It was all physics, but she was one heck of a storyteller.

Trick 2

IT'S NEWS TO ME

IN THIS FEAT of mentalism, your parents tell you where to cut from a newspaper or magazine and the selected words match your prediction.

Have you ever seen the following happen when your parent loses their glasses? They turn the entire house over, looking under every pillow, opening every drawer, and the glasses were on top of their head the entire time. Sometimes the answer to a problem is so simple, but people complicate the situation unnecessarily.

This mind-reading trick is one of my favorite effects to perform because the secret is so obvious if you know what to look for. The solution will be right under your parents' noses, but they won't notice it! This trick is bold, fun, and you won't believe you can get away with it.

YOU'LL NEED

- A newspaper or magazine
- Scissors
- Invisible tape
- A pencil or pen
- Paper
- Envelope for your prediction

THE SETUP

1. Cut a strip of newspaper or magazine. You can use any piece of printed material, as long as it contains a solid block of text. Make sure there is a clean line of text at the top. Write down this entire line on a piece of paper. Maybe it reads "in the spring when flowers". Put this paper in an envelope marked "PREDICTION."

Setup Step 1

2. Rotate your strip of newspaper 180 degrees so the text is now upside down. To enhance the illusion, next cut out a headline from the newspaper. You're going to tape this to the top of the strip, with the tape behind the paper so no one can see it. Now you have what looks like a normal newspaper clipping, but with the text upside down! Use your fingers to cover the space where the headline and text are taped together.

Setup Step 2

3. Take a few steps back so your parent can't get a really close look. They will see the large headline and won't focus on the smaller text. You are taking advantage of their selective attention!

PERFORMANCE

1. Point out that you've made a prediction and put it inside an envelope. You will go nowhere near it.

Performance Step 2

2. Next, hold up the newspaper. Run a pair of scissors up and down the length of the strip, asking your parent to tell you when to stop. It's best if they stop you somewhere near the middle, so don't bring the scissors too close to the ends.

Performance Step 3

3. Once they've said stop, you can ask them if you should cut a little higher, a little lower, or stay right there. Emphasize that they have free choice! When they've settled on the spot, cut the paper and let the cut portion flutter to the table.

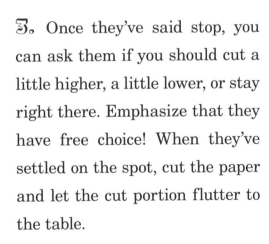

4. Have your parent pick up the paper and read the top line. What they don't realize is that this line was the original bottom of the upside-down newspaper. You could have cut anywhere! Of course, it reads "in the spring when flowers". All that is left to do is to admire your parent's flabbergasted expression as they open the envelope and see that the prediction matches their selection!

Performance Step 4

RICHARD TURNER (1954–)

RICHARD TURNER IS one of the world's best card mechanics. His performances consist of fancy shuffles and cuts, and despite mixing the cards, he can always deal himself the aces, a royal flush, or even put the cards back in their original order! Turner's abilities are particularly remarkable because he faces a significant challenge—Turner is completely blind. He fell in love with card tricks at age seven, but an illness caused his eyesight to deteriorate rapidly. However, that didn't stop Turner. He learned all the skills of the old "card sharps"—the gambling experts—and became one of the most skilled card technicians around. You think that's impressive? How about this: he's also a black belt in karate.

SPELLBOUND

YOUR PARENT HAS a free choice of eight objects in front of you. They close their eyes and spell—in their head—the name of the object. When they open their eyes, you've impossibly read their mind!

The best part of this trick is that you can come up with your own list. It's like you are designing your own secret code.

THE SECRET

Every object has a different number of letters in its name.

YOU'LL NEED

- A cup
- A book
- A plate
- A candle
- A stapler
- A calendar
- A lightbulb
- Headphones
- A wooden spoon for a magic wand

Notice these objects are three, four, five, six, seven, eight, nine, and ten letters long. You can substitute any object for one that has the same number of letters. For example, instead of a book, you can have a fork, and instead of a calendar, you can use a pine cone. Get creative! But whatever you choose, you must memorize the order.

THE SETUP

On the table, lay out these eight objects randomly.

PERFORMANCE

1. Show your parent that you've assembled eight objects from around the house. Say, "I have a plate, a candle, a calendar . . ." If you tell them the objects' names, they will know exactly what each one is called. This way they won't mistake a saucer for a plate or a novel for a book.

2. Tell your parent to think of any one of the eight objects and keep its identity a secret.

3. Next, say the following: "In a moment I'd like you to close your eyes and silently spell the object you're thinking of. Each time you hear a tap from my wand, say the next letter in your head."

You'll then demonstrate how this works by saying, "For example, if you were thinking of the cup, you'd silently spell C-U-P." As you say each letter, tap any three objects (but not the cup).

Performance Step 3

Then tell your parent, "And when you come to the last letter in your object's name, please say 'stop.' Okay?"

4. Now ask your parent to close their eyes and spell the name of their object as you tap. They think you are about to tap objects randomly, but what you're really going to do is tap them in the order of the lengths of their names.

Start by tapping any two objects. For the third, tap the cup. For the fourth, the book. And continue sequentially through the list of objects until they tell you to stop.

5. After they say stop, ask your parent to open their eyes. Your wand will be on the object they were thinking of!

126

ALIVE OR DEAD

BY HARNESSING PSYCHIC powers, you can detect a spiritual presence in your parents' written word. What I love so much about this trick is that the secret is so simple. But your performance will convince your parents that you are a powerful medium of the metaphysical. I'll also teach you a force that will make your parents think that *they* are in touch with the netherworld. They won't be able to explain it!

THE SECRET

It's not about the word. It's about the paper. A clever method of tearing allows you to keep track of which piece of paper your parent has chosen.

YOU'LL NEED:

- A piece of paper
- A pencil or pen

THE SETUP

No setup required for this trick. It can be done completely impromptu!

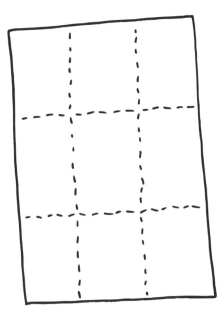

Performance Step 1

PERFORMANCE

1. Show your parent a blank piece of printer paper. Crease the paper by folding it into thirds and into thirds again. You now have nine sections of paper. Tear neatly along those lines and mix them casually. Make sure to keep track of the center piece and place it on top. How? Here's the secret to the whole trick: the center piece will be the only piece with four torn sides.

You can even have your parent tear the paper! Just keep your eye on that center piece.

2. Hand the center piece to your parent and ask them to secretly

write down the name of someone who is no longer living. It could be George Washington, Catherine the Great, or Mohandas Gandhi. Perhaps they write down Gandhi.

3. After your parent has written the name, have them turn the piece facedown on the table. Then give your parent the remaining pieces of paper and have them secretly write eight names of people who are living. They could be your next-door neighbor, your kooky uncle, or Zendaya. After they are done, they can turn them all face down and mix all nine pieces around on the table.

4. Announce that using psychic powers, you can figure out which name radiates a spiritual presence. Concentrate on the face down pieces of paper in front of you. Hover

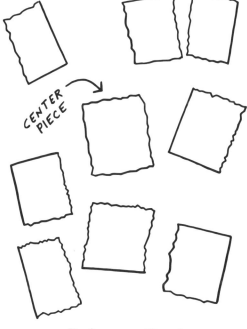

CENTER PIECE

Performance Step 4

your hand over each piece, sensing for "energy from beyond the grave." When you come to the center piece, announce that you feel a cold sensation! It must be this one! Turn it over and reveal that you've found Gandhi. As long as you spot the four torn sides, you'll never lose track of the center piece.

MAKE THE TRICK
BETTER

Some of the best tricks put the magic "in the hands of the audience." In other words, your parent will be the one who *somehow* locates the center piece. You'll accomplish this by using a cousin of magician's choice called the **PATEO force**, which stands for "Pick Any Two. Eliminate One." It's sneaky, clever, and will really leave your parent scratching their head.

PERFORMANCE

1. Explain that together you will make some psychic decisions. You will take turns doing the following: one of you will select two pieces of paper, and the other person will remove one of them. You'll go back and forth until there is only one piece left on the table. During all of this, continue to hover your hands over the

pieces so that you are metaphysically sensing their energies. Have your parent do the same. They are now part of the trick!

2. The secret? Make sure you keep track of the center piece and never eliminate it. Start by asking your parent to concentrate psychically and then point to two pieces. If they don't choose the center piece, you can eliminate either of them. If one of them is the center piece, you eliminate the other one, of course. Now it's your turn to feel the energy. Select two pieces that are not the center piece. Your parent can then choose to remove either of them. Continue going back and forth until there's only one piece left. Have your parent turn over the paper, see the name of Gandhi, and CRAAACK—their brain will break into a thousand tiny pieces.

HARRY HOUDINI (1874–1926)

WE ALL KNOW Harry Houdini as the most famous magician who ever lived. Born Erik Weisz, "The King of Handcuffs" became a household name because of his daring escapes. Houdini freed himself from prison cells, packing crates at the bottom of the river, even the belly of a dead "sea monster" (which was probably a 1,500 pound sea turtle).

But one thing Houdini could not escape was death. Houdini died on Halloween night in 1926. For the most part, Houdini did not believe that the living could speak to the dead. But that didn't mean he wasn't going to try. He and his wife, Bess, promised each other that whoever died first would try to contact the other from the Great Beyond. They agreed on a code word: BELIEVE. For ten years after his death, Bess held séances on Halloween night hoping Houdini would communicate this word to her. She never did hear from him, but still today people conduct séances on Halloween, trying to contact the great magician on "the other side." What about you? Do you believe?!

TRIPLE TELEPATHY

DISTORT YOUR PARENT'S sense of what is happening when by using one of the most closely guarded secrets in magic, the **one ahead** principle. This trick is so much fun to perform because you will always be one step in front of where your parent thinks you are. Isn't that how it always should be?

THE SECRET

Use one of your card forces so that you're secretly controlling one of three random choices. You will be "one ahead" of this choice.

YOU'LL NEED

- Three slips of paper
- A pen or pencil
- A deck of playing cards

THE SETUP

Decide what card force you want to use and put a force card on the top (Double Cut Force) or the bottom (Cross Cut Force). Let's say it's the four of spades.

PERFORMANCE

1. Begin this trick by announcing that you are going to use your telepathic powers to predict three of your parent's thoughts. First, ask them to think of any vegetable but tell them not to say it out loud.

2. Stare right into your parent's eyes, pretending to peer into their mind. Hold up a slip of paper (paper #1) and say, "I've got it!" Write down your first prediction without showing it. Secretly write down "FOUR OF SPADES." You are now one ahead—you'll see how shortly.

3. Then say, "Now that I've committed my prediction to paper, what vegetable did you think of?" Your parent will say something like "cucumber." You'll then declare, "Exactly what I predicted on this paper!" And point to the facedown slip of paper you just wrote on.

4. Next, ask your parent to think of any date from any year, like 1984 or 1527. Again, look into your parent's eyes and declare,

"I have it again!" Pretend to write down your prediction of a year on paper #2, but instead write down "CUCUMBER." As before, then ask them what date they were thinking of. They'll say "1885," perhaps. You'll respond, "Absolutely what I thought too!" and point to slip of paper #2.

5. For the third and final thought, have your parent choose a playing card. And you guessed it . . . you are going to force the card you wrote down before. You were *one ahead* with this card, and now you are going to catch up to it. Use the Cross Cut or Double Cut Force to have your parent "randomly" select the four of spades.

6. Have your parent look at the card and then gaze into their eyes. "Your card is . . . hmm . . . I see. Yes, I will write your card down here." And write down "1885" on slip of paper #3.

7. All that is left is to reveal that you successfully predicted your parent's choices! It's important to do so in the proper order: first show that cucumber was correct, then 1885, and finally the four of spades. A triple telepathic miracle!

MAKE THE TRICK
BETTER

You can perform this trick over Zoom, FaceTime, etc. As in A Force from Anywhere!, use the Cross Cut Force to force the bottom card of their deck. Also, for an added level of trickiness, try it this way:

PERFORMANCE

1. Have your parent show you the fan of cards so you can spot the bottom card. Then have them cut the cards for the Cross Cut Force, leaving the packet at a 45-degree angle. But this time don't have them look at the force card yet. Tell your parent you'll come back to it.

2. Just like above, ask them to think of a vegetable and write down "FOUR OF SPADES."

3. After they tell you it was a cucumber, ask them to think of a date and write down "CUCUMBER."

4. After they tell you it was 1885, now go back to the cards. They are on the table, already cut, with the four of spades ready to be forced. But you've just used the ultimate time misdirection. By now they've definitely forgotten which half of the cards was which!

5. Have them look at the force card and write down "1885."

6. Like before, reveal all three predictions in order and take your well-deserved applause.

DAI VERNON (1894–1992)

DAI VERNON (pronounced like "die") was one of the most legendary sleight of hand artists of all time. Born in 1894 in Ottawa, Canada, he became known as "The Professor" because of his great ability to teach magic. But Vernon first entered the history books at the age of twenty-six. In 1922, in Chicago, he showed a card trick to Harry Houdini. Houdini had long boasted that he could watch any trick three times and know how it was done. Vernon performed a card trick called The Ambitious Card and fooled Houdini again and again and again. From that moment on, Vernon became known as "The Man Who Fooled Houdini."

ANIMAL INSTINCTS

THE BEST MAGIC tricks use **multiple methods**, meaning they mix a bunch of different secrets together. That makes them very hard to figure out. Even if your parents crack part of it, they can't figure out the whole thing. This next mentalism effect combines math, puzzles, and magic to create a truly perplexing illusion.

THE SECRET

This trick uses both a mathematical force and some sneaky questioning to figure out your parent's choice.

YOU'LL NEED

· The chart of 100 emojis on the next page

51	61	71	81	91
52	62	72	82	92
53	63	73	83	93
54	64	74	84	94
55	65	75	85	95
56	66	76	86	96
57	67	77	87	97
58	68	78	88	98
59	69	79	89	99
60	70	80	90	100

THE SETUP

1. Snap a photo of the emoji chart or download it at www.howtofoolyourparents.com. Print it or show it on a screen. You can even create your own. Just make sure the animals below are in the squares numbered in multiples of nine.

2. Familiarize yourself with the following list of nine animals at the multiples of nine. You don't have to memorize their exact numbers.

9	36	63
18	45	72
27	54	81

PERFORMANCE

1. Ask your parent to pick a number in the following way:

 a. Choose a two-digit number, for example, 31.

 b. Add those two digits together. So, 3 + 1 = 4.

 c. Subtract that number from your original number. In this case 31 − 4 = 27.

What your parent doesn't know is that they will always have a number that is a multiple of nine.

2. Next, have them look at the chart and remember the emoji that is at the number they are thinking of.

3. Look deep into your parent's eyes and ask them to concentrate on their emoji. Say something like, "I'm getting a reading. . . . Yes, I have a picture in my brain . . . you are thinking of an animal!" Your parent will be shocked. So far so good!

4. All you need now is the first letter of your parent's animal and you will know which one of the nine they chose. As you continue to look into their eyes, say, "Can I please have just the first letter of your emoji?" If they say the letter "S," you know they chose the skunk.

5. The rest is all acting. And your goal is to make the trick seem more difficult. I chose the nine animals for this trick because there are many others in the chart that start with the same letter.

You can say, "Hmm, so it could be the snake, snail, shark, or squid." Point them out on the chart. "There are just so many!" Stare into your parent's eyes. "Think of your animal . . . it's cute, right? Well, sort of? I'm sensing a smell . . . . something that stinks. You are thinking of the skunk!"

Remember, it's important to be kind to your parent as they struggle to untangle the knots you just tied in their brain.

One of the nice things about this trick is that it works perfectly over Zoom, FaceTime, etc. After your parent selects a number, you can either screenshare the 100 emojis, text an image of them, or hold them up to the camera. All that remains is for you to stare into the screen and access their thoughts!

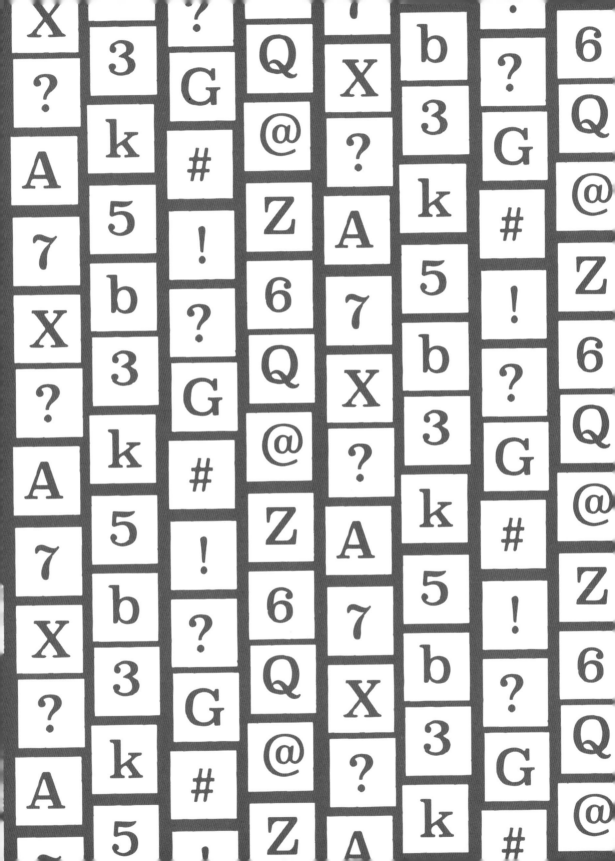

PART FOUR

COVERT
COMMUNICATION

"NOW YOU *SAY* IT, NOW YOU DON'T!"

IT'S NO SURPRISE that there is a close connection between magic tricks and secret codes. Both of them operate on the premise of "I know something you don't know."

When I was a kid, I had the most fun sending secret messages to my brother, right under my parents' noses. It's not that the messages were hidden. In fact, sometimes we would leave them on the kitchen table. But because our parents couldn't crack the codes, they had no idea what we were communicating to each other. For me, it was just like performing a magic trick. I was the one who got to set the rules and control what information my parents were allowed to have.

In this chapter, I am going to share six different ways that you can secretly communicate with a friend or sibling. Some of these techniques can even be used for magic tricks!

149

HARRY LORAYNE (1926-2023)

ONE OF THE smartest magicians ever was Harry Lorayne. He was an accomplished sleight of hand artist but was best known for being a memory expert. You've heard of an illusionist, a mentalist, and a hypnotist, but what about a mnemonist (*mnemon* means a unit of memory)? Lorayne was born in New York City in 1926. Even though he had dyslexia, that didn't stop him from becoming the world's foremost memory expert. Lorayne's big break came in 1958 on the game show *I've Got a Secret*, when he memorized the names of the hundreds of people in the audience. Lorayne claimed he could memorize the names of *thousands* people during a performance! How did he do it? He had a secret

system! He would associate articles of clothing with mental pictures. If someone named George had on a blue tie, he would picture George Washington wearing that tie. The human brain is better at remembering images, but that doesn't excuse you from finishing your English homework!

A SUPER "BASIC" INVISIBLE INK

THE HISTORY OF sending secret messages goes back thousands of years. The ancient Greeks would shave off people's hair, tattoo their bald heads, and let the hair grow back to cover the message. *Do not try this method*. But I have a suitable alternative for you, and it uses ingredients you can find around the house: baking soda and grape juice.

Baking soda is "basic" and reacts with grape juice, which is acidic. Here's your chemical formula: Base + acid = your parents won't have a clue what your messages are about.

Want double deception? Write your invisible messages in the secret codes you'll learn in this chapter. Good luck, parents!

THE CODE:

1. In a small glass or bowl, mix two tablespoons of baking soda with two tablespoons of water. This is your invisible ink!

2. Use your cotton swab to write your secret message on the paper. Allow up to thirty minutes for your piece of paper to dry.

3. Use a second cotton swab to "paint" purple grape juice over the secret message. Better yet, use a sponge or cotton ball to

paint with bigger strokes and reveal the message quickly. This works because baking soda is a base and grape juice is an acid, and when they are combined, they create a chemical reaction.

Step 3

WHY DOES INVISIBLE INK WORK?

ALMOST ALL LIQUIDS are either acids or bases. Grape juice and lemonade have a tangy taste. Fruit juices are acidic in nature. Baking soda, on the other hand, is bitter. If you rub it between your fingers, it feels soapy. That is its basic nature.

pH is the measurement of how acidic or basic something is. It's on a scale from 1–14. Things that are extremely basic have a pH close to 14. If there's a pH closer to 1, you have something extremely acidic, like hydrochloric acid. You don't want something like that around the house!

Whenever you combine an acid with a base, the pH of the total solution changes. But purple grape juice is special—it's both an acid and a pH indicator. A pH indicator is something that turns a new color to let you know the solution's pH has changed. If you used orange juice (an acid but not a pH indicator) instead, you wouldn't see a new color and your message would remain invisible.

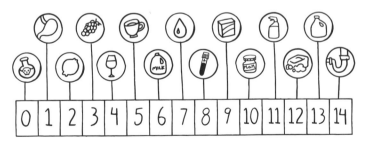

BOOK CODE

WITH A BOOK code, you will take your secret message and *encode* it using a specific book that you and your friend both have.

There have been many famous book codes in real life and in fiction. In *The Valley of Fear*, Sherlock Holmes decrypts a code using *Whitaker's Almanac*. In 1820, Thomas J. Beale, a devious Virginia gentleman, supposedly buried treasure and encoded its location with the Declaration of Independence. The Revolutionary War traitor Benedict Arnold disguised his secret communications using *Bailey's Dictionary*. But we all know how that turned out for him. . . .

A book code is one of the most difficult codes to crack (unless you're Sherlock Holmes) because someone would have to know exactly what book you are using.

THE CODE:

Grab a book and make sure your friend has the same one. Your code will consist of three sets of numbers. To encode a letter, find a word in your book that starts with that letter. Then indicate to your friend how to find that word with the three numbers. The first number will be the page, the second number will be the line, and the third number will be the word on that line.

For example, the letter "S" using the next page would be encoded like this: 157-1-5. That's page 157, the first line, and the fifth word (simple).

The word "SECRET" would be this: 157-1-5, 42-7-2, 91-5-2, 112-3-11, 131-1-9, 10-8-8.

The code is so simple, but because your parent won't have the key, it's virtually impossible to crack!

THE BEALE CIPHER

IN 1885, A pamphlet called *The Beale Papers* described how in 1820, Thomas J. Beale and a group of thirty men spent months mining gold, silver, and jewels from the western frontier and buried the treasure somewhere in a vault in Virginia. The value of the treasure today would be $43 million. Beale wrote three encrypted messages that described the location, the amount and value of the treasure, and the names of its owners. It was discovered that the second message was encoded using the Declaration of Independence, using the same system you just learned! Many people have traveled to Virginia and dug up farmland in hopes of scoring the millions. The other two messages have never been decoded, but they would certainly lead to the exact location. Do you want to give it a try?

Trick 3

MASONIC MYSTERY

THE MASONIC CIPHER is a code that is shrouded in mystery. A secret society, Freemasons (or Masons) have been in positions of power and influence for centuries. George Washington, Benjamin Franklin, and Paul Revere were Freemasons. Winston Churchill, Voltaire, and Mozart were also members. Freemasons communicated with each other using this code to keep their rituals and history secret. The cipher was so important to the Masons that some even engraved it on their tombstones! Who is a Freemason today? No one knows exactly. But if you come across their code, you will be able to break it!

YOU'LL NEED

- A pen or pencil
- A piece of paper

THE CODE:

The Masonic Cipher, or pigpen cipher, is a geometric substitution code. Each letter of the alphabet corresponds to a piece of the below grids. Dots are added for half the letters.

Copy the grids below onto a piece of paper or reference this book while you're encoding your message.

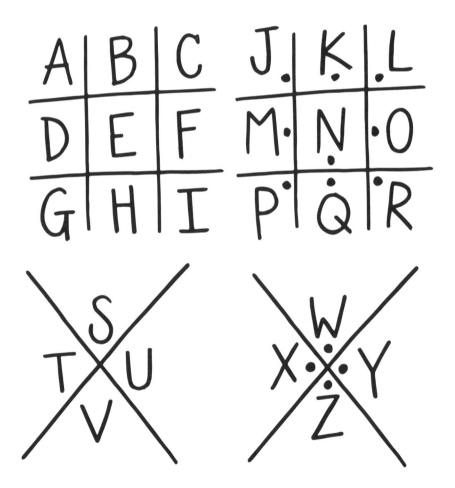

For example, here are the letters "B," "N," and "W."

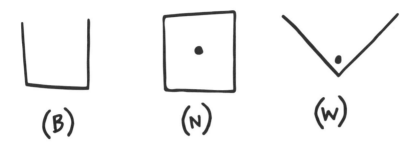

(B)   (N)   (W)

See if you can decode the below. And have fun!

JULIUS ZANCIG (1857–1929) AND AGNES ZANCIG (1857–1916)

THINKING ABOUT TAKING your secret codes to the stage? Then familiarize yourself with one of history's most legendary mentalist duos, the Zancigs. Julius and Agnes Zancig were billed as "Two Minds with but a Single Thought." In their most famous routine, Julius would go into the audience to borrow objects. He would ask Agnes, who was blindfolded, what he was holding. Without being able to see, Agnes could describe exactly what the object was. How did they do it? The Zancigs mastered a "code act." The specific words Julius used were codes for the information Agnes needed. For example, if "please" equaled "watch," Julius could convey to Agnes that he was holding a watch by saying, "*Please* tell me what is in my hand, Agnes." If he borrowed a wallet, and "next" equaled "wallet," Julius would ask, "*Next*, can you sense what this object is, Agnes?" The Zancigs were so proficient at their code act that they convinced the world they had telepathic abilities.

THE CAESAR SHIFT

THIS SECRET CODE was used by Julius Caesar, the mighty leader of the Roman Empire. Caesar was a military genius and encrypted sensitive messages with this code. Over two thousand years later, you're going to communicate secretly in the exact same way. The beauty of the Caesar Shift is that you can easily change your code if your parents catch on to you.

YOU'LL NEED

- Cardboard

- Two circular objects for tracing. A bowl and glass work great.

- Scissors

- Tape

- A ruler

- A pencil or pen

- A thumbtack and an eraser or a brass fastener

THE CODE:

1. Begin by tracing a large circle on your piece of cardboard using the outline of your bowl. Do the same with your glass for the smaller circle. Now cut out both.

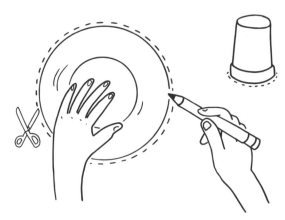

2. Place the smaller circle in the middle of the larger one and temporarily place some tape between them so they stick. You will remove this tape eventually.

3. Use your ruler to draw vertical and horizontal lines. Divide each piece in half until you have thirty-two pieces.

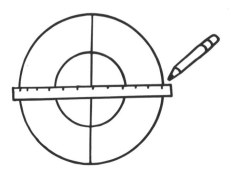
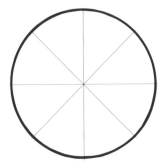

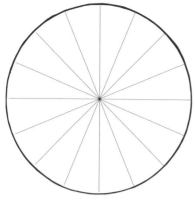
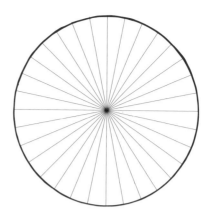

Step 3

4. Write the letters A–Z in each of the spaces. For the inner wheel, put lowercase letters. After you've put in the twenty-six letters, use the other six spaces for any punctuation you like. Maybe write ? ! . , : @

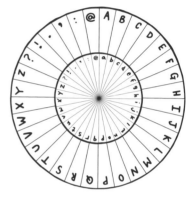

Step 4

5. Stick your thumbtack through the cardboard and use a pencil eraser underneath to cover the sharp end. If you can get your hands on a brass fastener, that works great too. Remove the tape so that you can rotate the smaller wheel.

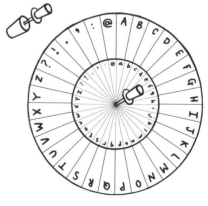

Step 5

6. Spin the wheel and choose a position. The inner wheel will contain the letters of your message; the outer will generate the code. In the image below, shift the uppercase letters forward seven in order to decipher the code. Thus, H = o, C = j, etc.

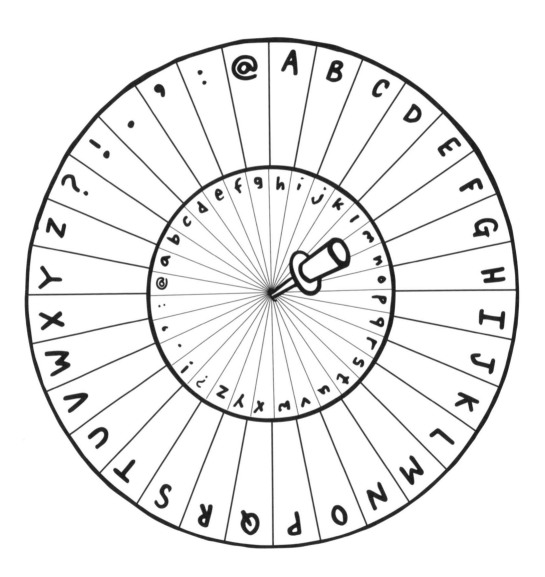

7. When you write your encrypted message, you have to tell your receiving codebreaker what code to expect. My favorite method is to include at the top of the page: "From the desk of Albert Einstein." This way your friend knows that the code is A = e.

Can you decode the note below?

I can fool you because you're human. You have a WONDERFUL HUMAN MIND that works no different from my human mind. Usually when we're fooled, the mind hasn't made a mistake. It's come to the WRONG CONCLUSION for the RIGHT REASON.

—JERRY ANDRUS

STEALTHY SIGNALING

THESE CODES ARE perfect for slyly transmitting numbers and letters to a co-conspirator. If you want to make them part of a magic trick, I suggest having a bunch of objects on the table. Your parents will choose an object while your friend is out of the room. When your friend returns, you can covertly communicate to them which object was selected.

YOU'LL NEED

• Objects on the table. For Code #1, you'll need an old clock.

• Your hands and feet

CODE #1–CLOCK CODE

1. Start by placing a bunch of objects, including a clock, on the table.

2. Ask your friend to leave the room. While they are gone, your parent will choose an object on the table. Suppose they choose the apple. Assist your parent in shuffling the objects around the table.

Make sure you grab the clock. You're going to turn its hands to indicate the position where the apple is. If the apple is in the third position, move the hands to 3:00.

CODE #2–HAND CODE

1. This is a great way to communicate a number. Have the objects on the table lined up from 1–10. You and your friend should agree that the left end is 1 and the right end is 10.

$\mathcal{2}$. After an object is selected and your friend returns, you can signal a number to them using the following method:

After placing your right hand on the outside of your leg for 1–5 or on the inside of your leg for 6–10, flash the appropriate number of fingers. For the eighth object (in the illustration on the opposite page, it's the banana), you would show a three on the inside of your leg.

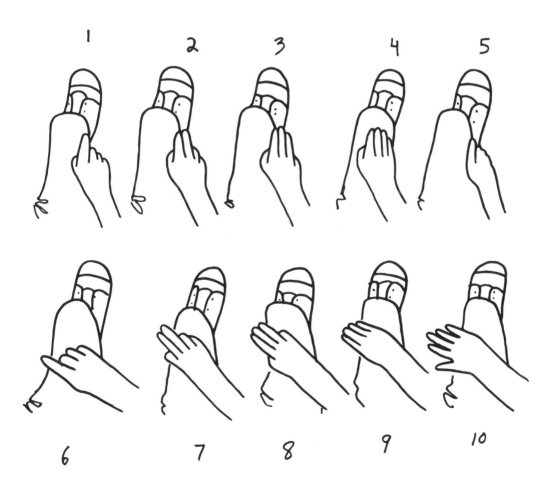

Use one hand per digit in a two-digit number. If your parent chooses the number 76 and you want to convey that to your friend, show a 7 with the right hand and a 6 with the left. Remember, your friend is looking at you, so they will interpret the right hand as the first digit and your left hand as the second digit.

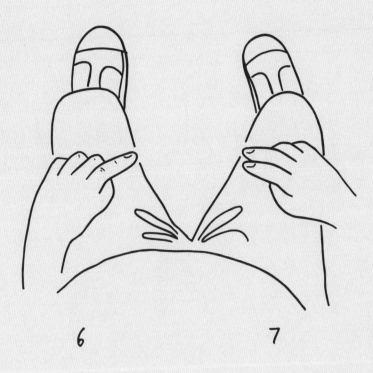

6   7

CODE #3—FEET CODE

Try conveying a number using your feet instead. If your right foot is the one that's pivoting, it's 1-5. If your left foot is pivoting, then it's 6-10. The angle of your foot indicates the exact number. For 3 and 8, neither foot is pivoting. Place your right foot ahead of your left for 3 and your left foot ahead of your right for 8.

1   2   3   4   5

6   7   8   9   10

ADELAIDE HERRMANN (1853–1932)

ADELAIDE HERRMANN WAS born in London to two Belgian parents. She was known as "The Queen of Magic," but this illustrious title did not come easily. For the first half of her life, Adelaide toured with her husband, Alexander Herrmann, and together they became one of the most successful magic acts of their time. But Alexander died unexpectedly in 1896, and suddenly Adelaide was staring at the end of her career. But Adelaide persevered, creating a solo act that took her throughout Europe and eventually to the bright lights of Broadway. One of her most famous illusions was Noah's Ark, in which she produced hundreds of animals on stage, including zebras, lions, tigers, and elephants. "The Queen of Magic" indeed! In the male-dominated world of magic, Adelaide Herrmann performed for more than fifty years before retiring at the age of seventy-six.

THE SECRETS OF SPARTA

COMMUNICATE WITH YOUR friends with an encryption method that was used by the powerful city-state of Sparta in ancient Greece! It's called a *scytale* (rhymes with "Italy"), and Spartan generals used this technique of hiding messages to exchange information about military campaigns. The key to a scytale is that only those with the same-sized cylinder will be able to read the message. So, make sure that your secret correspondent has the right-sized tube.

YOU'LL NEED

- Paper
- Scissors
- Invisible tape
- A ruler
- A marker
- A cylindrical object like a paper towel tube

THE CODE:

1. Begin by finding a cylinder for encoding your message. You can try rolling pins, flashlights, or even tennis racket handles. Paper towel tubes are a great way to start.

Setup Step 3

2. Cut strips of paper and tape them together. The thinner the paper strips, the longer the scytale's message can be. Just make sure the strip is long enough to cover the whole length of the tube.

3. Next, you're going to wrap the strip around the tube. Start by lightly taping one end of the strip to the end of the tube. Wrap the paper strip so that it completely covers the tube. Try not to overlap any of the paper.

Setup Step 5

4. When you're finished covering the entire tube, cut off any extra paper. Then tape down the other end of the strip so everything lies flat.

5. Now take your ruler and draw horizontal lines across the paper. Write your secret message from one end to the other. You can continue it onto the next line if need be. Then fill the rest of the scytale with random letters.

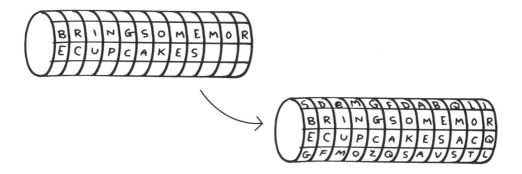

6. Last, unwrap your scytale and leave it lying around the house to taunt your parents.

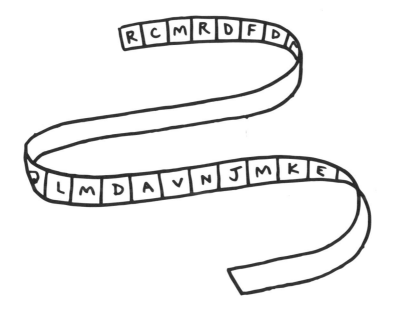

JOHN MULHOLLAND
(1898–1970)

WONDERING HOW YOU can put all these secret codes to work? John Mulholland was one of the leading authorities on magic, writing ten books and editing the *Sphinx* magazine for over two decades. In 1953, Mulholland was recruited by the CIA to advise on spycraft, secret codes, and mind control. On the next page is one of the methods he came up with for spies to communicate with each other. I wish I could share more, but much of his work is still classified!

SHOELACE SIGNALS

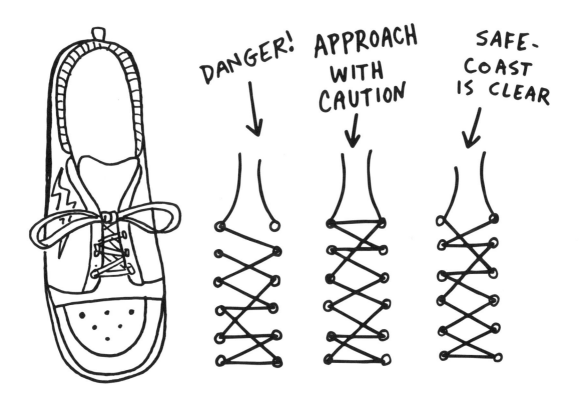

DANGER!

APPROACH WITH CAUTION

SAFE- COAST IS CLEAR

CONGRATULATIONS!

YOU'RE NOW ON the inside. You're the smartest person in the room. You know genuine magic secrets that have been handed down through generations of illusionists. Protect this confidential information with your life!

But I have one more secret to tell you: your parents *want to be fooled*.

Yes, they will be baffled and befuddled, but your parents can't help but recognize that you've practiced and mastered a special skill. A lot of work goes into a perfecting a magic trick or secret code, and when you fool your parents, they will be impressed with what you've learned.

Also, when people watch a magic show, they want to be

entertained by things they do not understand. Your job as a magician is to create astonishment and amusement *while* fooling people. Above all, magic should be about spreading wonder.

Even today, my favorite people to fool are my parents. When I'm creating miracles onstage, I love looking into the audience and seeing that same sheepish grin my father had at the pumpkin patch when I was seven. I know that he is confused, amazed, and proud at the same time. And *that's* the joy of magic!

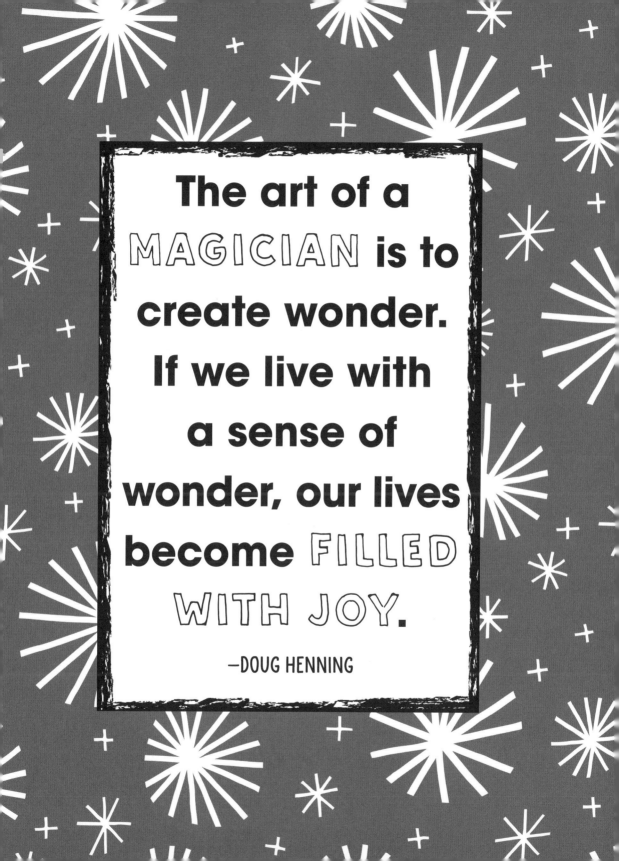

The art of a **MAGICIAN** is to create wonder. If we live with a sense of wonder, our lives become FILLED WITH JOY.

—DOUG HENNING

TOP SECRET!